Acting It Out

In *Acting It Out*, you'll discover how to use drama in your ELA and Social Studies classrooms to boost student participation and foster critical thinking. With years of experience supervising arts integration programs in Chicago Public Schools, authors Juliet Hart, Mark Onuscheck, and Mary T. Christel offer practical advice for teachers in middle and high schools. Inside, you'll find:

- Group activities to improve concentration, harness focus, and engage students of all abilities and learning styles in teamwork.
- Close reading exercises that encourage students to think critically and build personal relationships with the text.
- Strategies for integrating active approaches to dramatic literature, such as improvisation and scene work.
- Ideas for using dramatic literature as a springboard for studying history and interdisciplinary studies.
- Annotated reading lists that highlight each play's content and recommended uses in ELA or social studies.

Throughout the book, you'll also find handy tools such as reflection questions, handouts, and rubrics. By implementing the strategies in this book and allowing students to step into different roles from a text, you'll improve reading comprehension and energize your classroom!

Juliet Hart is the Director of Education at TimeLine Theatre Company. She has presented workshops on active approaches to drama in the classroom for the Illinois Association of Teachers of English and National Council of Teachers of English (NCTE).

Mark Onuscheck is the Director of Curriculum, Instruction and Assessment at Adlai E. Stevenson High School. He also serves as an adjunct professor at DePaul University.

Mary T. Christel is a former teacher of world literature, media and film studies, and theater. Currently, she contributes teaching resources to TimeLine Theatre's Living History Program and also reviews prospective lesson plans for the R

Acting It Out

Using Drama in the Classroom to
Improve Student Engagement,
Reading, and Critical Thinking

Juliet Hart, Mark Onuscheck, and
Mary T. Christel

Routledge
Taylor & Francis Group

NEW YORK AND LONDON

First published 2017
by Routledge
711 Third Avenue, New York, NY 10017

and by Routledge
2 Park Square, Milton Park, Abingdon, Oxon, OX14 4RN

Routledge is an imprint of the Taylor & Francis Group, an informa business

Library of Congress Cataloging in Publication Data
Names: Hart, Juliet, author. | Onuscheck, Mark, author. | Christel,
    Mary T., author.
Title: Acting it out / by Juliet Hart, Mark Onuscheck, and Mary
    Christel.
Description: New York : Routledge, 2017. | Includes bibliographical
    references.
Identifiers: LCCN 2016019697 | ISBN 9781138677432 (hardback) |
    ISBN 9781138677449 (pbk.) | ISBN 9781315559513 (ebk)
Subjects: LCSH: Drama in education. | Drama—Study and
    teaching. | Acting—Study and teaching.
Classification: LCC PN3171 .H275 2017 | DDC 371.39/9—dc23
LC record available at https://lccn.loc.gov/2016019697

ISBN: 978-1-138-67743-2 (hbk)
ISBN: 978-1-138-67744-9 (pbk)
ISBN: 978-1-315-55951-3 (ebk)

Typeset in Palatino LT Std
by Swales & Willis Ltd, Exeter, Devon, UK

You never really understand a person until you consider things from his point of view . . . until you climb into his skin and walk around in it.

Atticus Finch in *To Kill a Mockingbird* by Harper Lee

Creativity is putting your imagination to work, and it's produced the most extraordinary results in human culture.

Ken Robinson

Contents

Meet the Authors

Juliet Hart is a founding member of TimeLine Theatre Company, where she serves as Director of Education and appears regularly onstage. Juliet holds a Master's of Fine Arts (MFA) in Acting from The Theatre School, DePaul University. She began her career as an intern at The Kennedy Center, in the Education Department and for their Theatre for Young People program. Juliet has taught drama at Prairie State College and worked in many Chicagoland public and private schools as a teaching artist. She is actively involved with Theater Communications Group's (TCG's) Education Directors Group, and with Chicago Arts Educator Forum (CAEF). Juliet has presented workshops on active approaches to drama in the classroom for the Illinois Association of Teachers of English and the National Council of Teachers of English.

Mark Onuscheck is the Director of Curriculum, Instruction and Assessment at Adlai E. Stevenson High School, where he was also an English teacher and the Director of Communication Arts. In his current role, Mark works with academic divisions around professional learning, articulation, curricular and instructional revision, evaluation, assessment, social emotional learning, technologies, and the implementation of the Common Core. Beyond his work in high schools, Mark also serves as an adjunct professor at DePaul University, where he teaches classes in Creativity and in Corporate Social Responsibility.

Mark was recently awarded the Quality Matters Star Rating for his work in online teaching. He is a grant recipient from the National Endowment for the Humanities and recently co-authored *Process, Not Product: Proficiency-Based Assessment* (Solution Tree). In his spare time, Mark helps to build curriculum and instructional practices for TimeLine Theatre's arts integration programs within the Chicago Public Schools.

Mary T. Christel taught world literature, media and film studies, and speech at Adlai E. Stevenson High School in Lincolnshire, Illinois from 1979 to 2012. She began her teaching career there as a drama instructor, designer, and director. Drawing on her theater training at Northwestern University, Mary has contributed chapters to *Teaching Shakespeare Today* (NCTE), *Teaching Shakespeare into the Twenty-First Century* (University of Ohio), and *For All Time: Critical Issues in Shakespeare Studies* (Wakefield Press, Australia). From 2002 to 2012 she provided teaching materials related to the Chicago Humanities

Festival and from 2004 to 2005 developed lesson plans for the Theater History Initiative for the Shakespeare Theater Company in Washington DC. Currently, she is a regular contributor to online teacher resource handbooks for Chicago Shakespeare Theater and teaching activities for TimeLine Theatre's Living History Program. Mary also has edited and co-authored several books on media literacy.

Acknowledgements

First and foremost, we'd like to acknowledge the Chicago Public School (CPS) students, their teachers, and the administrators who continue to inspire our work and allow TimeLine Theatre's Living History Program to grow and flourish. Our TimeLine teaching team—past, present, and future—share their energy, ideas, and expertise with hundreds of students each year, inspiring them to take creative risks. And, Maren Robinson, TimeLine's Resident Dramaturg has been invaluable to us in the classroom and in developing our chapter on dramaturgy.

Thanks to everyone at TimeLine Theatre Company, for embracing the mission of the Living History Program and supporting its implementation. We appreciate being a part of the process of the Company's productions from the first rehearsal to the final student matinee.

Our work in CPS would not be possible without the support of Polk Bros. Foundation, The Crown Family, The Lloyd A. Fry Foundation, Robert and Eleanor Meyers, and John Sirek, as well as our "anonymous" donors.

For reading strategies and interdisciplinary curriculum development presented in this book, we recognize Ann Christiansen and Jane Gargaro for their insights and mentorship. Likewise, we would like to also recognize the great insights from the Literacy Coaches at Stevenson High School: Daniel Argentar, Brian Wise, and Maureen Rubenstein. Special appreciation goes to Shakespeare & Company, The Theatre School, DePaul University, and Christine Adaire for showing us how to explore active approaches in the classroom. And, we remember Anne Thurman, a creative dramatics pioneer at Evanston, Illinois School District 65 and at Northwestern University, who brought active approaches into ELA, Social Studies, and Science classrooms and inspired a generation of classroom teachers to follow her lead.

Finally, the three of us are grateful to have an opportunity to collaborate on this project which challenged our creative, analytical, and organizational abilities to transfer what we know works in our classrooms, what supports national and local standards, and what can be adapted to complement any existing ELA and Social Studies curricula. We are indebted to our patient and encouraging editor, Lauren Davis, who discovered the seeds of a book when she attended a presentation of activities included here at the annual convention of National Council of Teachers of English in Washington, DC.

1

Bringing Dramatic Literature to Life Through an *Active Approach*

What Does "Acting It Out" Really Involve?

The idea of allowing your students to engage in "acting it out" might seem a bit intimidating, especially if you haven't had firsthand theatre experiences yourself. But, are you familiar with the scenario of students sitting quietly at their desks reading and rereading passages from a text without increased comprehension or with much personal engagement? If so, you might be motivated to try some new approaches that demand deeper student engagement. In this book, we want to inspire you to take an *active approach* to working with dramatic literature in your classroom. This approach borrows techniques from an actor's toolkit and uses theater rehearsal methods to help students closely read a text, make personal connections to it, and work as a team to bring that text to life through classroom scene showings. We will share our experiences through the lens of TimeLine Theatre Company's Living History Program, an arts integration theater residency, which pairs non-fiction research and theater rehearsal techniques with reading dramatic texts to challenge students to "step into" another era or set of social circumstances. We have found, time and time again, that using simple, specific theater-based techniques to get students connected with their bodies and voices can breathe new life into studying plays. We hope that by the end of this chapter, you'll see that a well-structured theater-based unit can help you address Common Core Standards in an invigorating, creative, and surprising way.

Offering a Bit of Context: TimeLine Theatre Company and Chicago Public Schools Partnership

TimeLine Theatre Company is a professional Chicago Equity theater with a specific mission: *to present plays inspired by history that connect to today's social and political issues*. The company's education department partners with Chicago Public School teachers to create lesson plans that use drama to encourage students to make personal connections to history. For example, the pilot program featured a six-session, curriculum-based unit in an American History classroom and included a field trip to the theater for a production of *The General From America* by Richard Nelson. This play, set in the early, uncertain years of America's birth, illuminates the complex story of America's most famous traitor, Benedict Arnold. Using a combination of research, character analysis, and scene study techniques, students explored the conflicts, characters, and volatile atmosphere of the revolutionary war period. Our next partnership was with an English Language Arts (ELA) classroom that featured a unit on *Paradise Lost* by Clifford Odets, an intense family drama set amidst the social and economic challenges of The Great Depression. The work of Odets is non-canonical, but unique, since he provides one of the earliest examples of an American playwright using poetic, metaphor-heavy street talk. Odets' use of ethnic and urban speech patterns can be compared and contrasted to the way rap lyrics, spoken word performances, and slam poetry explore urban life today. These early partnerships in arts integration helped us understand which resources were most helpful to students and teachers, how to ask questions that complemented the class curriculum and supported Common Core Standards, and, perhaps most importantly, how to differentiate instruction for students of all abilities, with differing reading levels and English language skills.

TimeLine's mission of presenting theater inspired by history that connects to today's social and political issues was a natural fit for Language Arts and Social Studies teachers looking for curriculum-centric programming that encourages students to connect the dramatic work they study to the social and political landscape they live in. This model can work well in many classrooms, from ELA and Social Studies classrooms to interdisciplinary learning teams. The research element of theater complements the increasing importance of non-fiction texts in ELA classrooms and helps students come to a deeper understanding of the dramatic work. The exercises included in this book will show you how to engage students of all abilities and learning styles.

As students bring a text to life through rehearsal techniques, opportunities abound for rich classroom discussion. Students can actively explore universal themes that appear in ELA literary selections. We recently centered a unit in an ELA classroom around Aaron Posner's dramatic adaptation of Chaim Potok's classic novel, *My Name is Asher Lev*, the story of a young artist torn between his Hasidic upbringing and his passion for creating art. The class explored non-fiction material about life in a Hasidic community in New York City in the 1950s. Stepping into Asher's shoes pushed students to think about their own role within their family unit, how they would react to the restrictions Asher faced, and what they would be willing to sacrifice in order to be heard.

The following example demonstrates effective integration of current events, drama, and critical thinking in a Social Studies classroom. In the fall of 2014, as the events in Ferguson, Missouri continued to unfold, students at North-Grand High School worked on John Conroy's play, *My Kind of Town*, about Chicago's police torture scandal. The students were exploring issues of race in their Human Geography class and the play presented the opportunity to explore the motivations of different characters, with very different perspectives. Another ELA classroom at Perspectives Leadership Academy read the play as well, examining its literary themes. The two classes went on to host and facilitate a community discussion on police brutality, community safety, and relationships with law enforcement. Rather than interrupting a unit, this partnership extended its reach by bringing together two schools and community members to talk about issues that were affecting their lives on a daily basis.

Opportunities like these abound. Consider a current social issue you are interested in addressing with your students. There is very likely a play that can help you do that actively. Classic or canonical works usually have universal themes (*Antigone*, *The Crucible*, *A Raisin in The Sun*) that can be applied to many topical subjects, and contemporary works may allow students to enter worlds they can't currently access or tackle complicated subjects head on (*The Laramie Project*). We have included several lists of plays throughout this book that we think would ignite lively discussion and inspire active learning.

If you implement some or all of the exercises and techniques presented in the following chapters, we think you and your students will also develop skills that will make your classroom more congenial, creative, and exciting. You will learn how a cast of strangers becomes a team, which needs to happen in every classroom, every new school year. We talk about sharing energy as an acting ensemble as we rehearse scenes and as audience members when we participate in a theater experience. Students learn that theater is a live art and involves an interchange of energy between performer and audience member by performing scenes for each other. They learn how an audience's laughter or sympathy can and should help an actor focus, not distract them.

Modeling good audience behavior for each other's scene work is the final step in the unit and students see that a performance is complete only when the audience joins in the experience. As students explore scenes in small groups and then move towards a performance experience for their classmates, they will begin to understand some of these concepts. Using the actor's tools for script analysis, rehearsal, and performance you can create a meaningful, engaging classroom experience with your students.

Not Just in Drama Class: Using Active Approaches to Dramatic Literature in Any Classroom

An active, theater-based approach encourages students to step sideways into a character and explore what it feels like to inhabit the cultural and emotional "shoes" of a character living within a specific historical and social context dramatized in a play. This allows for a couple of things to happen. Students use a variety of close reading techniques to unlock clues in a dramatic text. Comprehension is a bridge to critical thinking about cultural and social differences in our world now and throughout time. In a later chapter we will show you some specific play reading strategies and also some that work well with non-fiction prose.

> In my opinion, most history lessons should be taught in such a manner because it is a wonderful experience to not only learn your history, but to act it out as well.
>
> —CPS Student

Once students understand deeply what they are reading, they can engage in rich discussion to explore their own feelings about history, and their place in it. So how do we start? Since we are teaching specific skills and vocabulary, we frequently choose four or five key scenes in the play to examine closely, rather than tackling the whole play. This allows us to create a mini-play that students are able to explore and understand on a deep level. You can then team this abbreviated version with a novel, story, or piece of non-fiction to explore related themes, conflicts, and characters. Imagine using a close reading of Langston Hughes' poem, "Harlem" to enhance understanding of Lorraine Hansberry's depiction of the South Side of Chicago in *A Raisin in the Sun*. We'll talk more in later chapters about how to develop a unit and create specific lesson plans that address the following questions:

- ◆ How do you read your lines closely in order to fully understand the playwright's intention?
- ◆ What homework must an actor do to understand the world of the play?
- ◆ How do you begin to develop a character?
- ◆ How do you effectively rehearse a scene with a partner?
- ◆ How do you develop a process for critique and revision of a performed scene with your peers?

Our units are structured to introduce and build skills as students progress through the scaffolded activities. We expect students to develop in the areas of speaking and listening, ensemble building, and play analysis. Each class, every day, begins with an appropriate warm-up activity designed to help students focus their attention and begin to recognize how to best work together as a group. We will show you some easy and effective warm-ups later in this book that will work well at the beginning of almost any class to foster teamwork, focus, and risk-taking. In subsequent chapters, we will present how to work with students in small groups in order to rehearse selected scenes or speeches, but, for now, realize that rehearsal requires teamwork (or ensemble work, as we call it in the theater), imagination, risk-taking, and revision. As students begin to share their work with each other in scene showings, they learn how to give and receive positive feedback and constructive criticism. Teachers that we work with, and students themselves, point to these skills as "transferrable"—in other words, once a drama unit has ended, the ensemble that has come together, stays together. One teacher noted:

> This group of students is particularly congenial in class as a result of building an ensemble. They are much more likely to give each other criticisms and prompts that are helpful than they were before. The students really liked coming to class to work on dramatic readings and their enthusiasm for unlocking the treasures of literature has extended into our next unit . . . They are willing to explore and discuss the motivations of the characters in the manner that [they learned]. The students now approach literature with more purpose and interest because they experienced it directly through dramatic reading.

They make discoveries about themselves and each other, and that has a positive impact on the general classroom environment.

Students also expand their understanding of not only the play, but of other varying content areas like history, science, math, current events, geography, cultural studies, psychology, and music. Arts integration at this level raises a student's awareness that art is a form of human communication and expression, and it forces questioning, reflection, and critical thinking. We hope that the play is just the beginning of an ongoing discussion and learning journey. Our goal is to ignite curiosity about history and current events and how they unfold, and to inspire students to seek more information, and perhaps even take action.

In other words, we see a play as a jumping off point. Your classes could move on to write their own scenes and adaptations. Your students could facilitate group discussions. You can use a theater-based project to inspire analytical and argumentative writing assignments that continue the critical-thinking process that started with the rehearsal process. We'll address some of these ideas and activities later in the book. But, maybe most importantly, the activities we talk about in this book make learning fun! You and your students will have a lot of laughs together as you navigate theater games and scene work. We hope that you will enjoy making discoveries about your students and yourself as you use them.

> The most memorable aspect of the program has been the bond it has created—between the individual students and myself . . . the program emphasized the ensemble in acting.
>
> —CPS Teacher

Opportunity for Reflection

Consider how you might apply ideas from this chapter to your own classroom.

1. Do you shy away from texts that you think might be too difficult for your students?
2. Do you consider ways to abridge the work? How would deep reading of key scenes from a play be just as helpful as reading the whole play out loud as large group?
3. What are your goals for a unit incorporating a play as a primary or supplemental literary text?
4. What is the role of current events study in a typical ELA classroom? How does that focus provide more "relevant" texts and topics for examination?
5. How much attention do your students pay to what is happening in the news? What are the issues that you think most affect the

community in which your students live? Have you considered giving your students an opinionaire at the beginning of the school year that allows them to target issues and events of interest and importance? How would students be more likely to engage in discussion after using this pre-assessment tool that targets topics that they identify as significant to them?

6. What prompts can you give students to encourage them to connect personally to the main ideas in the play? How might sharing the responses to these prompts be done in a way that encourages ensemble building?

7. Consider the personalization that takes place when students embody a character. What is it that makes one student's choices different from another's? How willing are your students to bring something from their own lives to a characterization? What kind of risk-taking does that involve?

2

Engaging Students: The Key Ingredient

Student engagement is an educational challenge. Educators know *what* students should learn and *why* students should learn. Our conversations about curriculum rationales and standards answer those challenges. But the more difficult questions continue to stand out: *How do students learn? How* do students learn differently? *How* do we engage students to capture their interest and imagination, while also developing their higher-order critical-thinking skills? Keeping these instructional questions at the forefront of our work reminds educators to pay close attention to the value of student engagement in relation to mandated learning standards. An *active approach* to learning enlivens curiosity, builds collaboration among diverse viewpoints, and fosters inquiry along with skill development.

This pedagogy assumes that engaging the learner is as important as learning, and creativity is critical thinking. Engagement not only builds "readiness," it builds high interest and curiosity—qualities that motivate students to investigate, make connections, purposefully reflect, and handle difficult topics. Students become engaged in real events, interpretation, analytical reading and writing skills, and thoughtful, debriefing discussions among their peers. This approach was created with educators and teaching artists from TimeLine Theatre's Living History Program working together to build highly interactive classroom environments and highly interactive thinking.

To start, we want to be clear about how the instructional strategies shared in this book are best practices for critical thinking and skill development. First and foremost, we want to re-envision how to approach rigorous expectations with rigorous teaching and learning practices. We also want to stress that active approaches to learning are highly adaptable. The purpose of the book is to focus on student engagement as the key to reaching every student. This vision is the basis for each of the following educational objectives. In this chapter we will look at *how* this is done, and we hope our work will help educators think differently about engaging teaching and learning.

Make the Connection: Engagement and Standards for Learning

Our best educational dialogues commit to developing students' critical-thinking skills. This focus cannot be repeated enough. Students should be demonstrating critical thinking every day in every classroom. At this point, we'd like to share our model's objectives as they directly support the Common Core Standards established for English and Language Arts and the C3 Framework recently published for Social Studies teachers. As these national standards are interwoven, these same objectives and instructional efforts connect with seemingly unrelated topics like Science and Mathematics, because they articulate relationships to thinking processes, argumentation, close reading, and cultivation of grit and perseverance. Our objectives drive instructional commitments to support these varied and interconnected learning standards. For the purpose of making those connections clear, we'll explain the way the program objectives connect to standards for teaching and learning. In this model, we are working toward the following five objectives:

1. Students cultivate new engagement strategies to discover the historical context of a play and the student's personal connection to it.
2. Students perform a section of the play studied in front of their peers that demonstrates their understanding of the context of the scene within the play.
3. Students develop a process for revision through constructive peer critiques and suggestions to improve the scene performed.
4. Students understand how reading or viewing supplemental fiction and non-fiction can support a deeper understanding of a play.
5. Teachers develop a creative, active approach to fulfilling Common Core Standards for ELA and Social Science classrooms.

At this point, we'd like to examine the value of each objective and explain its depth, value, and alignment to Common Core Standards.

Exploration Through Rehearsal

Objective 1: Students cultivate new engagement strategies to discover the historical context of a play and the student's personal connection to it.

The main purpose of our approach is to help students make a personal connection to dramatic texts: the play's world, characters, and themes. In this way, students examine their own current, lived experiences. The range of topics TimeLine's Living History Program plays tackle, provide students with dynamic, high-interest content, from the more widely taught work of Arthur Miller's *The Crucible* to more contemporary plays that go unread in many high schools such as Larry Kramer's *The Normal Heart*. We've supplied examples of plays that interest students that include canonical and non-canonical titles and playwrights at the end of each chapter.

Creating personal and meaningful connections to stories is one starting point for fuller engagement. Readers and audience members must discover a way to connect to a story. They must find a reason to listen and to watch a play in order to follow the progression of the plot. We cannot overlook that learning how to connect with a story is its own skill. Educators know this, and they work with instructional strategies that build these personal connections. They begin their teaching in a way that helps students empathize with a character or in a way that captures student interest. This personal exploration of "connecting" is an early stage of the rehearsal process, and it is embedded in the program's journaling exercises, classroom warm-up activities, discussions, questioning strategies, and explication of the text. Through these methods, you can an align activities and assignment expectations to the Common Core in ELA and Social Studies.

Understanding a Part in Relation to the Whole

Objective 2: Students perform a section of the play studied in front of their peers that demonstrates their understanding of the context of the scene within the play.

Fundamental to students' reading ability is whether they actually *understand* what they've read. This skill cuts across all disciplines and is a surprisingly difficult task for many readers—many of whom demonstrate varying strengths of understanding based on subject matter, genre, and complexity. For instance, a student may comprehend fiction better than non-fiction, or may comprehend a history book more easily than a science book. They may understand one and not the other. Or, as reading specialist Cris Tovani identifies, students may perform the action of reading, but they don't "get" what they've read (*I Read It, But I Don't Get It: Comprehension Strategies for Adolescent Readers* [Stenhouse Publishers, 2000]). After reading, students may convey little understanding of a text. Some, as we are aware, can convey no understanding.

"Reading for understanding" is a priority in our instructional approaches to teaching and learning, and given the varying abilities of literacy skills in schools, we work attentively with teachers to teach complex texts effectively. Here, differentiated instruction can take hold in a way that makes thoughtful instructional sense with the Common Core. To this point, differentiated instruction is attentive and willing to vary the content of learning, the process of learning, and the products that demonstrate learning.

In terms of content, scene selection allows for greater differentiation for varied abilities in reading. Teachers can select scenes and character parts that can most appropriately challenge students in relation to articulated standards for learning. Likewise, the non-fiction readings can vary in complexity, offering more summary-based supports about history, issues, events, and time, or offering more sophisticated readings that can push stronger readers to their fullest potentials.

As noted earlier, process is also a function of differentiated instruction. During the rehearsal process, students are introduced to a range of innovative reading techniques that help every student to gain greater traction behind their comprehension. Many of these activities allow students to concentrate on differing elements of a scene or character development, by constantly adjusting the reader's focus and concentration. At times, this process may involve vocabulary building skills, explication of quotations, or the sequencing of lines and words that build toward a progression of meaning.

In meeting this objective, students create and perform an actual scene from the play. Moreover, students build an underlying and enduring skill that is of greater value. They learn to make stronger, associative connections between "a part" of a text and the "entire text." By learning a character part, students are expected to describe how the role fits into the larger context of the play; or, by learning a scene, students are expected to be able to state how the lines contribute to the progression of the play's plot line. For any reader, this skill is significant. It demonstrates how the reader comprehends a text, follows the development of a text, and how a story and its characters evolve.

Continuous Improvement Is a Learned Skill

Objective 3: Students develop a process for revision through constructive peer critiques and suggestions to improve the scene performed.

Seeing and re-seeing from multiple viewpoints is an important learning skill. It helps students to build up a commitment to continuous improvement and life-long learning. We come together to learn from one another, from the rich diversity of what we are, where we come from, and how we think. This commitment builds collaboration, generates diverse feedback, and places great emphasis on reflection and revision. These educational commitments hit on why we come together as learners, and they are modeled in our lessons. Our model works with the process of collaboration, feedback, reflection, and revisions on a number of valuable levels that reflect the vision of the Common Core. The rehearsal process of a scene becomes a dynamic experience for students, which helps them to see learning as a constantly developing, changing, or refining process in more specific and vivid ways. When we address "critical thinking" we are addressing how students develop minds that are attentive to subtleties and distinctions as they build better interpretative choices, better acting choices, and better insights into the characters' stories. These insights depend on the value of multiple viewpoints in discussion, viewpoints that challenge one another and viewpoints that assert themselves. Nowhere is this more important than in discussing the history that shaped us. The rehearsal process makes this level of discussion a deliberate one, allowing for input that brings every student's story into the play's story.

Relevance of Research and Supplemental Print and Non-Print Texts
Objective 4: Students understand how reading or viewing supplemental fiction and non-fiction can support a deeper understanding of a play.

The twenty-first-century learner must be able to conduct research in a way that sorts and selects pertinent information. This means a student needs to develop a process that helps to evaluate and judge how to filter the vast amount of material that is available during this "information overload era." For many students, this process is completely overwhelming. During the research experience, they struggle to sort and select information that will be most valuable to support their understanding of history. In some ways, this is similar to an actor's situation when faced with a play that takes place in a very specific time and place. Actors need to know what information will be most helpful to them as they "step into the shoes" of a character. A dramaturg helps an actor with this work as the actor begins the rehearsal process. One of the many functions of the dramaturg is to produce a body of research for the actors and the director, almost acting as a production's librarian. The classroom dramaturgy work, as we will describe in Chapter 6, would involve selecting non-fiction reading and viewing experiences that add clarity to the historical context of the play, how that particular history was constructed, and how the history was experienced and conveyed.

This kind of research not only helps students create a picture of the specific world of the play, but students also begin to generate the analytical ability to understand history as it is recorded in history books as comparison to how it is explored in plays. Looking at historical fiction, primary sources,

non-fiction, and visual texts side by side inevitably creates powerful analytical comparisons and contrasts. Developing these skills leads students to
demonstrate their understanding of varying viewpoints and how bias influences the way history is portrayed or magnified, or how it is misleading and
misunderstood.

Uniting Creativity with the Common Core

*Objective 5: Teachers develop a creative, active approach to fulfilling Common Core
Standards for ELA and Social Studies classrooms.*

Our work supports the efforts of educators working to implement the
Common Core Standards, specifically in ELA and Social Studies. This work
is done in partnership, and it is meant to fulfill the variety of skill require-
ments teachers are working to incorporate. This objective is about striving
to implement standards effectively and in a way that is highly engaging to
student learning.

The Common Core Standards not only articulate a vision of continuous
improvement, they orientate a vision of collaborative learning and instructional best practices in academic disciplines. Moreover, they better state
the way disciplines overlap and, if interwoven, the way schools can build
high-order, critical-thinking, and skillful students. Academic disciplines do
not exist in silos; skills in one academic area are deployed or nuanced in
other academic disciplines, too. For instance, every subject teaches literacy.
Likewise, the capacity of building an argument is equally important in Social
Studies as it is in Science and Mathematics. Students benefit when school
curricula are organized in a way that recognizes this level of overlap because
skills become reinforced throughout the day instead of viewed as stand-alone,
isolated experiences.

Empowering Learners: Long-Term Outcomes

Clear and definitive research around the value of the arts in nurturing
learning continues to grow. At this point, the mounting evidence supporting arts education is inarguable. The fine arts—music, visual arts, theater,
dance—belong in a student's school schedule. The value these courses bring
to student attendance rates, social emotional learning, and development of
mathematics, writing, and reading skills is indisputable, not to mention the
long known fact that art has value for art's sake alone. Whether your school
has a robust arts program or not, our approach will help you access the tools
an actor uses that can ignite a complex learning process. While reviewing the

lessons and reflections of the artists, teachers, and students featured in this work, we hope the following three outcomes are made vividly clear:

1. Students can transfer the theater skills and information they have learned about the cultural, social, and emotional world of the text/play to other areas of learning.
2. Students engage in collaboration and written reflections, about how their view of history or a social issue has been changed by studying and working on this particular play.
3. Students can explain the relevancy of research and reading both non-fiction and primary source material to better understand the context surrounding a dramatic text.

As this book unfolds chapter by chapter, we hope we can make the interconnections between the value of the instructional practices and the development of the theater-based skills we value for student learning and development.

Opportunity for Reflection

Consider how you might apply ideas from this chapter to your own classroom.

1. Considering these objectives, what would the students be doing differently from more traditional classroom environments? What would that engagement look like and sound like?
2. How would your engagement with students change with an active/physical approach to a text? How can you encourage students to take risks? What would that look like and sound like?
3. In considering how students are engaged differently, what skills are they practicing that are of value? Why do you view these skills as valuable? In what ways are they important to teaching learning?
4. How do these objectives relate to students' different abilities? Can you see how differentiated learning can happen fairly easily?

3

Opening Up the Classroom Actor's Toolkit: Promoting Student Engagement Through Active Approaches

Bravo! You have decided to embark on a theatrical adventure with your students. Rather than reading a play quietly to themselves or even aloud from their seats in the classroom, your students are going to take an active approach to a play, as a group of actors would. Initially, you may play the part of the director, at least as you kick off this unit. As students become more comfortable with new activities and skills, they may take on some of these responsibilities. As they learn to work together, your students will become an ensemble, which is at the heart of any theater experience—or any collaborative classroom activity. Simply put, an ensemble is a group of actors that have come together as a team to create a piece of theater. Building the ensemble experience in your classroom early in the school year can help create an environment that combines hard work with play, discipline, and trust. When those elements come together, you have a classroom that promotes creative risk-taking and deep discovery. This chapter offers activities and techniques that will help harness focus, build concentration skills, and reward cooperation. Using these activities regularly within a structured unit will reinforce these key concepts and help students see improvement in very specific skill areas. We will then introduce a close reading approach for working on a monologue that your classroom ensemble can tackle together before they begin working on scenes in smaller groups.

How to Build an Ensemble

An active approach to ELA instruction may or may not be new to you and your students. The activities in this book depend on use of the body and the voice, which in turn requires vulnerability, risk-taking, and practice. That's asking a lot from students who may be shy, uncertain, or uncomfortable speaking English. But if the class agrees as a team that this approach will be a challenge, that it will encourage them to take creative risks together, and that it will support all members of the ensemble as they try new things, the payoff will be great and lasting. Not only can students expect speaking, listening, and focus skills to improve, they will see their peers in new and possibly surprising ways. As one student put it, "I see a different side of my peers when they play a character that is very different from who they are."

Introducing Classroom Actor Basics

Student will have to learn a few "actor basics." These activities will challenge students to be "actor ready." In all of these activities, we begin in a circle, which encourages everyone in the ensemble to be able to see each other and make eye contact. In that circle, we'll ask students to:

◆ Assume an actor ready position: Stand up straight, don't lean on anything, keep feet hip distance apart, with your arms hanging relaxed at your side.
◆ Be able to take a good deep breath into your belly from this position.
◆ Only use your voice when it is part of the activity; otherwise, find energy in the silence of the group. This will help the group focus on the task or activity at hand.
◆ When we do speak, we speak as loudly as we can. As actors, an audience has to be able to hear us.

Once students have those basic performance norms in mind, they are ready to engage in ensemble building warm-up activities.

Activity #1: Just Say, "YES"

In order to get the whole room to buy into this ensemble mindset, we like to begin each new residency with an activity called "YES." If you are at all familiar with the rules of improvisation, you'll know that the golden rule when improvising a scene is to say "yes." Why must we say "yes" in the theater or in improvisation, and why is it great to say "yes" in the classroom? Well, if a performer is improvising a scene with you and that fellow performer presents you with a situation (you can imagine anything . . . a wild animal in the back seat of your car, a box of melting ice cream cakes, a wild request for help), and you say "no," what happens? The scene dies. It has nowhere to go. Sound familiar? The same thing happens in your classroom when a student refuses to engage for whatever reason. Showing students the power of "yes" encourages them to take a risk and make the choice to *engage* with you and with each other. This activity is ideal because it immediately reveals the transforming power of "yes."

Activity Instructions

Step 1. The class forms a circle.

Side-coaching suggestion: Ask students if they understand why "yes" is an important word in improvisation. If they don't know, use the explanation above to explain why.

Step 2. Student A begins in the center of the circle. They need to make strong eye contact with another participant, Student B, and say their name loudly and clearly. If the name is correct, Student B says, "Yes!" Student A then begins to move into Student B's spot, while Student B moves to the center, makes eye contact, and names another participant, Student C. Student C says "Yes!" and Student B begins to move to Student C's spot in the circle.

Step 3. The game continues to be repeated in this fashion until everyone has been named and said "Yes." Once participants understand the process, the game can speed up. An individual should not move until they have been rewarded with a strong "Yes!" from the person they are pointing at.

Side-coaching suggestions: If Student A calls Student B by the wrong name, Student B does not say "No." Instead, Student B says their correct name. Student A repeats the correct name, with eye contact, Student B says "Yes", and the round continues. Ask your students what happens when someone says "No." The flow of the round stops, progress stops, and the person who has said the incorrect name feels silly or embarrassed. When that person receives the correct name by their fellow ensemble member, they feel like they can trust the ensemble. If they make a mistake, someone will help them out, and together, we can accomplish the goal of the game. As students get stronger in their ability to focus on each other, and make strong eye contact, and once everyone learns each other's names, they can move on to other levels of the activity.

◆ Variation #1: This version is the same minus the naming. Student A makes eye contact with Student B. Student B says "Yes!" and makes eye contact with Student C while Student A moves toward Student B's spot (as in the basic approach) and the game pattern continues.

◆ Variation #2: This version is now played silently using only eye contact and the established movement pattern.

This activity may seem simple but it is a highly effective concentration and ensemble building game. Students are required to focus on each other, practice speaking clearly and keep the game moving forward by saying, "Yes." Once the students have agreed to say "Yes" to the ensemble, they can work on making the ensemble stronger and more effective.

Sharing Energy and Building Trust

As a teacher, you take the temperature of your classroom every day. Are the students bouncing off the walls, or barely awake? What you will be able to accomplish that day can depend a lot on the energy in the room. When you are establishing an ensemble with your students, one goal is to create an even and effective energy in the room. If we could start every class with the following game, we would (and we often do). After one round, you'll see where your class is that day, and if you use it repeatedly, day after day, not only will you establish a routine that helps get everyone on the same page but you'll see concrete improvement in focus, speed, and teamwork. A routine that encourages disciplined engagement can signal to your students that it's time to commit to the ensemble, and leave everything else at the door.

Activity #2: Pass It Along

Activity Instructions

Step 1. The ensemble stands in a circle. Explain that we will be passing a single clap around the circle. That single clap represents our shared energy. Choose one student to begin. Student A faces the person to their left (Student B), makes strong eye contact, and claps. Student B must anticipate this clap, and clap at the same time. In other words, we are passing the clap by clapping simultaneously.

Side-coaching suggestion: Maintaining focus and eye contact is crucial to executing this seemingly simple, coordinated action.

Step 2. Student B, who has received the single clap, then turns to the next person in the circle and passes the single clap to them. Student C receives it in the same way, by facing the giver and clapping their own hands at the same time. In this way, the clap moves around the circle in one direction.

Side-coaching suggestion: The goal is to establish and maintain a consistent rhythm and to practice active giving and receiving.

◆ Variation #1: After participants have mastered passing the clap in one direction, introduce the option to change the direction of the clap. In order to do this, the person receiving a clap can choose to clap a second time, reversing the direction of the clap. In this case, the goal is for the person giving the clap to then seamlessly become the person receiving the clap and to keep the game moving forward.

◆ Variation #2: You can also introduce a second clap into the circle. At some point a student may receive a clap from two different directions. What do you do in this situation? That is up to the student, and to the ensemble. They will quickly discover that yelling at each other, or berating each other in that situation does not help the game move forward, but quick thinking, creativity, and teamwork will solve the problem.

In this game, students have to think on their feet, just as an actor has to think quickly when something goes wrong on stage (which it very often does). This activity heightens the necessity for attentiveness and staying connected, as well as learning to read subtle non-verbal cues and reacting quickly.

The rhythm of the clap is the heartbeat of the ensemble. The ensemble will want to keep a strong, steady heartbeat—they don't want to flatline, or go into cardiac arrest!

Making Body and Voice Connections

It's a fact that students today are plugged into technology a lot of the time. Conversations, altercations, and declarations can take place entirely electronically and face-to-face interactions are becoming less commonplace. But as a classroom becomes a rehearsal room, we are asking students to make strong connections with each other using their voices and their body. These strong choices are what make a scene come off the pages of a book and roar into life. The stronger and bigger the choice a student can make, the more exciting the scene is for the rest of the class to watch. Be patient. It may take a little work to get your students comfortable using their voices boldly and using physical actions to portray their characters.

Activity #3: Sound Around

This activity combines sound and gesture, and is also a lot of fun. Once students have built the necessary focus with "YES" or "Pass It Along," you can follow it up with "Sound Around," which will warm up the voice, body, and imagination. You'll see that students may need a little practice to get creative with their choices, but after a few rounds, it will happen. Again, just be patient, and watch what evolves after some practice. The discoveries students may make in this game can be carried into the rehearsal process later on. Generating sound and movement as an ensemble can be also be incorporated into that work. Students may find ways as an ensemble to create organic sound that adds tone or mood to a scene. This activity depends on the ensemble to pass energy around the circle: this time in the form of a sound and a gesture.

Activity Instructions

Step 1. Have students form a circle. Student A begins by making a sound and a gesture at the same time. For example, Student A waves both hands, saying "Whoosh." The sound and gesture then gets passed around the circle, each student doing their best to imitate the original sound and movement.

Step 2. Once the sound and gesture makes its way around the circle and have "returned" to Student A, Student B begins a new sound and gesture that make their way around the circle and the activity continues in that manner.

Side-coaching suggestions:

○ Encourage students to use different levels of sound, different kinds of sound, and eventually to combine emotions with their sounds and gestures (like a shocked gasp, with the hands covering the eyes).
○ Depending on the size of your class and the amount of time you have, you can choose to go a quarter of the way around the circle and pick up the next day with the next quarter.

This activity encourages students to use their voices creatively and assertively, and it allows students to practice specific gestures, which will come into play much more as we begin to rehearse scenes in small groups.

Activity #4: Trippingly Off the Tongue Twisters

Here is another advantage to using acting techniques and warm-ups in the classroom: as your students work together to bring a text to life, they can't help but see how important articulation and volume are to the task at hand. These skills, along with increased confidence, translate directly to success in everyday life and students know this. The activities thus far have centered on focus and volume. Next try adding articulation to students' skill set. Select some favorite tongue twisters or a poem to warm up the articulators: facial muscles and the lips, teeth, and tip of the tongue. Those selections should be easy to remember, so students can use them as a warm-up any time they are faced with speaking in public.

Activity Instructions

Step 1. The activity leader begins this exercise from the center of your classroom circle, using call and response.

Step 2. Say a tongue twister (see suggestions below), and have the students repeat it together as a group.

Step 3. Start slowly and quietly, and, as the articulators warm up, you can increase the volume and speed.

Step 4. The leader also can play with accents and tone of voice.

Here are some favorites that work well, and move quickly:

"The lips, the teeth, the tip of the tongue."

"Unique New York, New York's Unique, You Know You Need Unique New York."

"Whether the weather is cold, or whether the weather is hot, we'll be together, whatever the weather, whether we like it or not."

"Will you?

Will you wait?

Will you wait for Winnie and Willie, the worldwide welterweights?"

"To sit in solemn silence in a dull, dark dock,

In a pestilential prison, with a life-long lock,

Awaiting the sensation of a short, sharp shock,

From a cheap and chippy chopper on a big black block!"

Activity #5: Strike a Pose for a "Tableau"

Through the pre-rehearsal work suggested so far, students are moving closer to working on scenes in smaller groups. This process will require shared creativity, collaboration, cooperation, and revision. Since students have spent a fair amount of time working as a full group, they can transition to spending some time in smaller groups of four to eight participating in an exercise called "Tableau." You can use this premise in many different ways: to explore the big ideas in the play, the history in the play, specific events in the play, or current events or headlines that relate to the themes of the play. Tableau depends on use of the body and gesture, and can incorporate sound as well. In a tableau, students will create still images with their bodies to represent a scene.

Activity Instructions

Give each small group of students a theme to explore (for example, greed, revenge, sorrow, love). One by one, each student steps into the performance area and establishes a still image in relation to the student next to them until the picture is complete. The scene can also be brought to life through improvisation, with the teacher clapping his or her hands to signal the beginning and end of the action.

Side-coaching suggestions:

◆ Feel free to adapt this exercise in many ways. You can also use newspaper headlines or a line from the play you will be working on to inspire the tableau.

◆ After each group has worked out their tableau, have students share with the entire class. Now you can begin to model constructive peer feedback. Ask students to respectfully share what they can see happening in each tableau by responding to the following questions:

  ○ What is happening in the tableau?
  ○ What else would you like to know about this tableau?
  ○ What do you think could happen if the group revised their tableau?

◆ After receiving peer feedback, each group can comment on how that feedback compared with their initial intentions for the tableau.

As you adopt these warm-ups or active bell ringers, having a wider range of activities adds variety to the routine and refines specific skills. Viola Spolin's *Theater Games for the Classroom: A Teacher's Handbook* (Northwestern University Press, 1986) provides a rich resource for expanding your classroom's bell ringer toolkit, and demonstration videos of those games will eventually be posted at spolingamesonline.org. See Appendix C, "Recommended Resources" for more books to have on hand.

Creating a New Approach to Bell Ringers and Redirection Strategies

These five activities help develop a particular set of skills: teamwork, trust, expression, risk-taking, and articulation. Again, these skills need not and should not exist in a silo, but can become central to your teaching pedagogy. Activities that build those skills will resonate immediately with kinesthetic learners as suggested by Howard Gardner's research on multiple intelligences (*Frames of Mind: The Theory of Multiple Intelligences* [Basic Books, 1993]). Introducing basic active approaches in any classroom can set a positive tone for learning and help redirect a class that struggles with behavioral issues, loss of focus, or just plain old fatigue. For example, if you begin each new term with the "YES" game, you are not only setting up expectations for participation and engagement, you'll also encourage your students to learn each other's names, which will help establish an ensemble feeling in your classroom, no matter what your lesson plans are. If you use "Pass It Along" at the beginning of each class prior to more traditional bell ringers that keep students in their desks, you can inject a dose of shared focus and uniform energy into your classroom. Students are more likely to focus on reading, writing, listening, and speaking activities. If you are working with a block schedule, an activity like "Pass It Along" or "Sound Around" will reenergize and redirect students midway through the period. A University of Illinois study from 2009 suggests that physical activity may increase students' cognitive control—or ability to pay attention.

Beyond Bell Ringer Ensemble Building Activities: Exploring a Monologue

The work you and your students have done together on ensemble building, voice–body connections, and articulation will pay off as you dive into the text of a play for the first time. In the following activity, students have the experience of working on a monologue as an actor would by using close reading skills and critical thinking to deconstruct the text. Through this activity, they will explore how vocabulary and diction shapes characterization, drives the plot, and reveals thematic ideas. By examining the monologue in isolation, students will begin to articulate the relationship between a monologue and the fuller play in which it resides. As their understanding of the monologue is shaped in this way, students interact dramatically with the text in order to explore character traits, choices, and themes of the monologue, both physically and vocally. Students are experiencing the text, not just "reading" it.

Activity Objectives

- Students will clarify any unfamiliar vocabulary in the monologue and explain how word choice informs an understanding of characterization and plot line.
- Students will be able to articulate what is happening in the monologue and how it connects to the fuller play.
- Students will be able to flesh out the overarching themes and ideas of the play.
- Students will begin to physically and vocally perform the monologue—exploring the motion and emotion of a character.
- Students will be able to reflect on their experiences, state the reasons for their acting choices, and discuss the possibility of differing choices among actors.

Walter Younger's "Proud" monologue from *A Raisin in the Sun* nicely illustrates how this monologue activity works.

The monologue:

Well, Mr. Lindner. We called you—because, well, me and my family—well—we are very plain people—I mean—I have worked as a chauffeur most of my life—and my wife here, she does domestic work in people's kitchens. So does my mother. I mean—we are plain people. And—uh—well, my father, well—he was a laborer most of his life—

And my father—My father almost *beat a man to death once* because this man called him a bad name or something. Yeah. Well—what I mean to say is that we come from people who had a lot of pride. I mean—we are very proud people. And that's my sister over there—and she's going to be a doctor. And we are very proud.

What I am telling you is that we called you over here to tell you that we are very proud and that this—Travis, come here. This is my son and he makes the sixth generation of our family in this country—and we have *all* thought about your offer—

And we have decided to move into our house—because my father— my father—he earned it for us, brick by brick. We don't want to make no trouble for nobody or fight no causes—and we will try to be good neighbors. And that's *all* we got to say about that. We don't want your money.

Activity #6: Group Monologue Work

Getting Started

Step 1. Ask your students to form a large circle. Each student receives one sentence, no matter how long or short, from the monologue on a piece of paper. We like to use cardstock and a large font, so that the words really leap out to the students. The individual sentences or "lines" are distributed in order around the circle.

Step 2. Students are asked to read their line and to identify any unfamiliar vocabulary words in their line. Unfamiliar vocabulary can open up a discussion about differing meanings and definitions of words as they help us to understand a character's thoughts. Students are then given a few minutes to memorize their line.

Step 3. Going around the circle, each student performs their line of text. Encourage your students to listen carefully to the line that comes before theirs and to begin to understand the emotion expressed in that line.

Step 4. The first round performance is mainly for the sake of memorization and confidence building. During the second round, each student must invest the line with the feeling or emotion that he/ she thinks the line implies. Going around the circle again, each student states what he/she thinks the play is about based on the line he/she memorized. The group performs the monologue around the circle, each student responsible for his/her line. Repeat this process until the monologue is fluent.

The Next Level

Step 5. Once fluency is achieved, encourage your students to add a gesture to the line as they say it, much like in "Sound Around."

This will help show how physical action can inform how a line is read or interpreted. Different physical actions will produce different line readings.

Step 6. Give students the full text printed monologue. Ask them to read it and annotate it, looking for clues to explain how the monologue might relate to the entire play.

Here are some questions to guide students' discussion of the monologue's meaning that coordinate well with Steps #4 and #6:

○ Can someone explain what is happening in this passage?
○ What are the main points of the passage?
○ Who thinks he/she has the most important line? Why?
○ How does punctuation influence which words and ideas are emphasized? How does it give the actor clues about the character's state of mind? For example in Walter's monologue, there are many, many dashes.
○ If you think of a monologue as a piece of music: Where does it rise? fall? become quiet, loud, slow, fast?

Throughout this activity, we like to stress that at this point in script analysis, there are no wrong choices, just choices. If you have time to allow several students to perform the same monologue, the class will clearly see how different each interpretation can be. And, if students are being true to their own experiences and true to the words on the page, those different interpretations are all valid and acceptable. If you can get to that point, then your class is in great shape to move onto scenework mapped out in Chapter 5.

Fostering "Buy In" and a Classroom that "Connects"

In this chapter, we've addressed how to begin to bring your class together as an ensemble, how to warm up the voice and the body, and how to create an atmosphere where creative risk-taking is encouraged and rewarded. The chapter's activities help students to focus and to say "yes" to new ways of working together. Now it's time to introduce some of the challenges that come with bringing a play to life, off the pages, and into the world of the classroom. In Chapter 2 we asked: How do students learn? How do students learn differently? How do we engage students to capture their interest and imagination, while also developing their higher order, critical thinking skills? Later, we'll address why plays may be particularly effective for student engagement because they ask students to step inside the shoes of a character to embody a dramatic conflict, and explore relationships between characters. But, for now, realize that when we embark on implementing active approaches to investigating a dramatic text, we are asking students to share part of themselves through the acting process.

Opportunity for Reflection

Consider how you might apply ideas from this chapter to your own classroom.

1. How do you think different kinds of learners will react to an active approach in the classroom?
2. How do you develop a collaborative spirit in your classroom? How are those skills introduced and cultivated?
3. Do you use bell ringers in your classroom? What form do those bell ringers take? How would incorporating your favorite bell ringers get students into the mindset of the play? And, how could they be combined with "active approaches" bell ringers?

4

"The Play's the Thing": To Read or Not to Read Dramatic Literature

Why Read a Play?

As Shakespeare wrote, "The play's the thing." Plays bring stories to life and engage the imagination. They bring us together as a community, and they pose questions around central themes about humanity, conflict, and social concerns. Moreover, they highlight the effect of choices as those choices are sequenced towards a resolution—whether that resolution is tragic or comic. And so, we read and watch plays to experience how characters interact to solve conflict.

In this chapter, we want to make three quick points: Point one, don't read a play like a textbook, like a novel, or like a non-fiction article. Point two, students don't need to read an entire play: select meaningful and colorful excerpts, scenes, or monologues that fit in with your lesson or unit. Point three, use plays to engage participation and to challenge students to read and think more critically.

Let's start with point one. Plays require a different approach to how we read than do textbooks, novels, or non-fiction. Plays require much more from a reader because they are not completely spelled out sentence-by-sentence, description-by-description. Most plays are all dialogue and occasional stage directions, so they leave a lot of room for interpretation and portrayal. This latitude offers students the opportunity to explore varying ideas and interpretations and connect those with how they see, hear, and feel the story. We think this offers both ELA and Social Studies classrooms a curious and more vivid learning experience.

Point two: Plays are easily segmented. A classroom doesn't need to read an entire play to gain insight into a viewpoint or alternative viewpoint. We know how much time it takes to read an entire play with a classroom word-by-word. Instead, we encourage teachers to summarize segments of the play and only read the scene or scenes that are most crucial or engaging to students. Select meaningful scenes that are directly connected to the learning targets for a lesson: a monologue, a dialogue exchange, a longer excerpt, or a few select scenes or exchanges of a play. By incorporating these passages within a unit of study, a lesson can provide a more enriching reading experience that heightens the critical thinking of students.

Point three: Beyond our immediate and long standing reasons to attend a play, teachers in ELA and Social Studies classrooms know that plays enliven a classroom and make students think more critically. Educators know that plays have an immediate appeal for students because they demand an active approach to teaching and learning. Plays are to be performed. When taught thoughtfully and with instructional intentions, teaching with a play should demand that all students participate in both the performing experience and learning experience of a play. In classrooms like these, teaching and learning breaks away from traditional, isolated reading routines. Plays require interaction and an active approach to learning. Don't read a play like a textbook.

In the Living History Program, we work with plays because they put students in touch with accessible themes that are reflected in literature, and they help students better understand the multiple viewpoints around social issues and the function of history. The reason we read plays is to investigate these viewpoints and to engage in dialogue around standing themes within humanity, how we grapple with conflict, and how different voices and viewpoints in history can be heard and revisited. We work with plays so that students can stand in history, relate to history, interact with history, and have a say about history, because we believe they need to learn to have a say in history.

Act One: Start by Addressing Accessible Literary Themes

When we read plays with our students, we need to connect the play to the student, not the student to the play. Plays address messages and meanings, and it is up to the teacher to zero in on what that message is—one that will awaken interest in students.

We suggest working with the accessible literary themes that run throughout a play and configuring ways in which students connect with those accessible themes of: love, revenge, pain, sadness, loss, fear, wonder, hope, death, pity, humor, confusion, or bad timing, etc. The key entry point for the readers' role in a play is to enter into it thinking, "Hey, I've felt that way, too. I can relate to that message." Or, "I've dealt with a similar situation." Students must access these themes from the start. They must find the relevance to their own lives. The job of good teaching locates the common ground between the text and the student.

When we work with plays, we are asking students to step into another character's shoes. They are asked to step into the minds of a variety of characters. Working with the themes embedded in plays allows students to speak someone else's words and perform someone else's actions as the character wrestles with the conflict. When students are given the opportunity to do this, they gain a heightened awareness of how others struggle with the same universal themes; they develop a sense of empathy, and they connect with conflicts that are relevant to their own experiences. This is an important aspect to both the ELA classroom and the Social Studies classroom. Students need to be able to "stand in the story" and "stand in history." When they are given this opportunity, they are able to study the story and the history from other viewpoints.

Reading Strategies to Consider: Accessible Literary Themes

We'll reiterate: a play is not a novel, a short story, or a piece of non-fiction. When we read plays, we need to approach them differently. Unlike novels or short stories, the author of a play does not provide every detail and description to the reader to guide them. Instead, a play focuses on dialogue and may provide an occasional cue or stage direction. Other than that, the dialogue is it. It is important to recognize this because plays are built only on what the characters say, so there is a lot of room for filling in the rest of the picture. To begin "filling in the picture," start with reading strategies that motivate students' understanding of the themes or messages within a play. Knowing the themes within a play can help students to manage their understanding of the conflict within the play, how that conflict is resolved, and how the characters interact to address the conflict. Here are a few reading strategies to help students to enter into the literary themes. Consider them and consider ways in which you can alter the activities to connect with plays you teach.

1. *Build personal connections:* Better readers configure personal connections to a story. Provide students with a journal prompt or activity that gives them the opportunity to relate their own experiences with the themes from the play. For instance, if the theme is "revenge," have students write about a time in their lives when they or someone they knew "took revenge" on someone else. Ask them to sequence the events and the consequences of their actions.

Or, if the theme is "loss," ask students write about a time they lost something: what was it, why did it mean something to them, and the feelings they have about missing it? Or, it could be a theme about love or a message about pity. The idea is that students get a chance to tell about their own experiences with the theme first.

A note about personal reflections: Always give students a way to participate. If they don't have a story from their own lives or if they are uncomfortable sharing a story from their own lives, have them write about a television program, a movie, or a news story they know about; then, have them explain how the theme was managed.

For example, when reading *The Crucible*, connect students by exploring their experiences of being "falsely accused." In reading a play like *Julius Caesar*, connect students by exploring their experiences of feeling "betrayed."

2. *Connecting quotations:* Better readers are able to pull important quotations from a reading and recognize how they build up the message(s) of a story. Plays are boldly expressed. As a way to connect readers to the themes, pull out key quotations from throughout the play that manage the development of the theme. A teacher can model this during Act One of a play by pulling out the major quotations and asking students to explain how the quotation is connecting to the fuller play or to the social studies topic being addressed.

   For example: When reading *A Raisin in the Sun* or *Clybourne Park*, select quotations or exchanges from the play that reveal the human feelings behind segregation.

3. *Literal and interpretative:* Better readers recognize the literal, and they search for meaning through "interpretation." Have students create a short original script:

   > With a partner or in a small group, have students create a short play about a theme. The play can be very short (25–50) exchanges between characters, but the play must introduce the theme, how the conflict builds, and how the conflict is resolved.

   For example: If reading *The Diary of Anne Frank*, have students develop their own dialogue of two or more individuals in hiding and in distress. Within the exchange, a conflict must develop and be resolved.

4. *Empathy and thinking from multiple viewpoints:* Better readers not only relate to their own understanding, they read to stretch their

understanding to a higher-order, more critical level. When we read history plays, students have the opportunity to be anyone in the play that is like or completely unlike them. This is a fun experience for students: to be a king or a queen, a die-hard romantic, or a villain or hero. Plays offer students an array of varying viewpoints. Step into those minds when you are reading a play or watching one. Ask: "Would I do that? How would I manage that? What might I say to that?"

For example: If reading plays like *The Normal Heart* or *The Laramie Project*, focus in on the injustices of being a victim of prejudice. How might it feel to stand in someone else's shoes? How might that victim be thinking or feeling? Why?

5. *Graphic organizers:* Better readers create and organize their thinking while they are reading. Many students find it difficult to keep track of a theme as they are reading a play. Provide them with a graphic organizer that helps them to trace the development of a theme over the scene and acts within the play. Provide them time to stop and to reflect on how it is developing. Or, give students an opportunity to predict what is going to happen next and why they are thinking that way.

For example: Give students a handout with six large empty squares on it like a cartoon strip or storyboard. In each box, student partners should retell the important part of the scene by drawing a picture of characters in key actions, provide the scene a title above the square, and provide a key quotation below the square. Then, have them share with the class.

Act Two: Build Critical Thinking Around Social Issues

Connecting students with accessible literary themes is a great starting point. In the work we are doing in schools, it is equally important for educators to connect students with the relevance of their learning and the development of their critical-thinking skills. ELA and Social Studies classes should connect students to the relevant social concerns that engage students' interests, and then they need to connect those concerns with the insights that can be drawn from a reading. When we work with multiple types of reading, both fiction and non-fiction, we are better able to draw a relationship between learning and the importance of learning.

In the work we do, we seek to build thinking skills with our students. Working with engaging curricular content connected to socially relevant topics to students allows those skills to emerge and flourish. Seek out plays and content that will have relevance to students, student learning, and student interest. Work with plays that connect students to social issues that are mean-ingful to them. When we do this, students have opinions that they want to share, allowing them to work with higher-order, critical-thinking skills like judgment, evaluation, and creating an argument. In this way, students get the chance to enter into the conversation, have input, and weigh the judgments of others.

Reading Strategies to Consider: Connecting to Social Issues

1. *Building interest and empathy:* Better readers know how to connect new readings with prior knowledge, interests, or experiences. To do this in an explicit way, bring in a "high interest" news story from a current event or ask students to locate news stories that are immediately relevant to the theme(s) the play addresses. Read those news stories and compare and contrast them to how the characters in the play are thinking or managing similar conflicts. As students read and discuss, pose guided questions that connect to this higher-level thinking skill. Ask students to explain their comparisons or their contrasts.

   For example: When reading *The Crucible*, have students locate articles related to famous "false accusations" in history. Or, for a play like *Julius Caesar*, have students find newspaper articles about political scandal or betrayal. In this way, students begin to see the ongoing, universal themes that plays reveal.

2. *Sorting and selecting details:* Better readers are able to identify more important details in relation to the major events of a developing story. They are able to explain why the detail was significant to the event or the understanding of a character. When we think about our understanding and the shaping of social issues, we must look at how details contribute to our understanding of the issue in small but important ways.

   For example: As students are reading, ask them to list and describe details in a play as they interconnect with the bigger events at work outside the immediate action of the play. For instance, in *"Master Harold"... and the boys*, which details help students to understand status of the play's three characters based on the South Africa's apartheid policies?

3. *Compare and contrast:* Better readers compare and contrast stories. Remember plays and longer works do not need to be read in their entirety. The more important skill is for students to be able to compare and to contrast perspectives. Plays are easily segmented, so it is often interesting for students to read an excerpt from

different reading about the same topic. Choose reading or viewing experiences that can be compared and contrasted and that allow students to debate the merit of each of the various viewpoints. Chapters 6 and 8 will provide a range of activities for this purpose. *For example:* If reading plays like *The Laramie Project* or *A Raisin in the Sun*, have students read positions around gender identity or race from different periods in time. Ask students to compare and contrast how viewpoints have changed or stayed the same.

4. *Questioning strategies:* Better readers are "questioning" while they are reading. When we read history plays, we usually ask questions like who or what is allowing this to happen and why? With questioning, get at the literal first. Ask, "What is happening in this scene or at this moment in the play?" Then, follow up with another question that forces the students to stretch their thinking in another, more thoughtful direction.

    For example: When students are engaging in an initial "table read" of a scene or later are acting out that scene, stop the scene. Ask, "What's happening right now?" Then, ask follow up questions, "What do you think the characters are feeling? Why?" Or, "What does the character want or need? Why do you think the character is struggling with right now?"

5. *Sequencing:* Better readers follow the sequence of events within a story and recognize how they are building. History plays most likely follow a chronological sequence. Discuss with students how each sequence is building and how events are escalating. In this way, students can begin to see the cause and effect relationships in history, and they can begin to make judgments about how important their own role is in the development of history.

    For example: In plays like *My Kind of Town, The Crucible,* or *The Laramie Project*, have students identify how early events begin to snowball into more upsetting and tragic events. When do they first start to notice that problems are mounting? How or what could have stopped the escalation of events? Why was the escalation unstoppable? How do we prevent similar events from ever happening again?

Act Three: Create and Recreate Historical Perspective

Plays centered around historical events, significant people, or important time periods should be approached differently from plays where the historical context is not central to the story's development. The major difference in reading a history play is that the reader/viewer often knows how the play is going to end before it begins, unlike other plays where the reader/viewer does not maintain that advantage. For these reasons we can examine history plays for other reading purposes and build greater, more varied critical-thinking skills within our students.

When we read or view historical plays, we develop insights about the history we've read in other non-fiction texts. We critically examine the irony of historical developments, the contradictions, the bias, or the particular viewpoints surrounding that period, event, or individual.

History plays demand a higher level of critical-thinking skills, and teachers should build lessons that challenge students to engage in higher-order discussions and interpretations that guide the growth of these skills. Making use of stronger reading, questioning, and discussion techniques open up those critical-thinking discussions.

Reading Strategies to Consider: Examining History Through a Play and Excerpts

1. *Read with a purpose:* Better readers read with a purpose in mind. They know what they are looking for before they begin to read, and they read with an intention. Struggling readers find it difficult to set a purpose for reading. In these cases, teachers should provide that purpose.

   For example: A teacher might simply say, "In scene two of the play, everyone should be able to describe each character's motives around the developing conflict." Or, a teacher might say, "As we are reading this excerpt, I want you to tell me how the character's thought process changes." Of course, there are many ways to establish a purpose: some very specific, some more general. Either way, a better reader comes at a text intentionally.

2. *Developing a critical perspective:* Better readers are always developing opinions, ideas, and judgments while they are reading. As they read they are evaluating and constructing a critical perspective. They might read and gain a different viewpoint or see and root out bias. Likewise, they might gain insights into a vivid historical understanding. Allow students to "act out" these differing perspectives.

   For example: Allow groups of students to rehearse the same or different scenes from a play like *The Crucible* or *Raisin in the Sun*. In their performance, they must present the character with differing interpretations of the character. Then discuss each group's portrayal of their scene. Or, have the student audience ask the actors to stay in character and answer questions like, "Why do you think that character said . . .?" Or, "How do you think this character would judge . . .?" These types of exchanges open up many thoughtful and provoking discussions.

3. *Reading for contradictions:* History plays allow the reader/viewer to pay attention to the sequence of events that lead to the resolution. As we read or view them, we should pay attention to the key moments and details within a play that are pivotal to the conclusion of the events. These are very important checkpoints for questioning and discussion activities. How do you think that detail or statement influences the outcome? What is ironic about what the character said earlier in the play?

   For example: Better readers review the reading they do. In a play like *My Kind of Town* or *The Crucible,* have students identify what they view to be the contradictions that emerge within the conflict and explain why they view these as contradictions either to the conflict in the play or to our contemporary mindset.

4. *Making current, relevant connections:* History is repeated because the themes in history are universal. Since this seems to be a clear pattern in history, identify non-fiction and other fictional excerpts that draw an immediate relationship between current events and the historical developments unfolding in the play.

   For example: If the theme of the play is corruption, have the students (or you) identify news stories with the same theme. Examine different forms of corruption. Or, make those personal connections to the play's text and to local, national, or global events.

5. *Drawing conclusions and a wider viewpoint:* Better readers work to answer the question "so what"? Why does this play or this discussion about a play or reading matter? Ask that question regularly and often. Students need to make associations to their learning and to the reason behind reading. Plays are a rich resource because they launch questions from differing perspectives, helping students to create a broader worldview.

   For example: Open up discussions as students are reading, have them trace the development of their viewpoint over the course of their confrontations with varying viewpoints. In what ways are their viewpoints reinforced? In what ways are viewpoints allowed to shift and to change. What accounts for a shift in viewpoint on an individual level? Or, what accounts for larger cultural shifts in belief systems?

Plays are rich and inventive reading experiences. As we work actively with students, we recognize the value of smart reading strategies that help students to understand both the literal and inferential meaning operating in the text.

Often, this effort means writing out guiding questions, which we refer to when working with students in active classroom lessons. We ask a lot of questions so there is absolute understanding and a foundational clarity to the text. This clarity and coherence allows us to build our students' more critical-thinking skills, and allows us to work with the nuances of characters and scenes. As we work alongside students, we are then able to tease out the more masterful inferences of an author's intent, and students are better able to convey that subtext in their acting and voice inflection. This level of close reading enriches the experiences of students, as they are being forced to think critically on their feet.

Opportunity for Reflection

Consider how you might apply ideas from this chapter to your own classroom.

1. How will I know if my students are developing reading skills?
2. In what ways can I structure my unit so that literary themes, social concerns, and history work in relation to one another and in a way that complicates thinking?
3. Whenever possible, how can I get students to collaborate over their interpretations and presentations of the play?
4. In what ways can assignments work together to visibly demonstrate that a student's reading and writing skills are developing to the greatest potential?

5

Acting It Out: Applying Active Approaches to Scene Study

In Chapter 3, we outlined how to begin building an ensemble atmosphere in your classroom, which encourages students to say "yes" to creative risks, to collaborate on drama-based activities, and to commit to clear communication skills, especially projection and articulation. Now it's time to jump into the deep end by exploring the text of the play though a student-friendly rehearsal approach. In this chapter, we will explore how to apply close reading strategies to uncover the playwright's themes and clues to character development, how dramaturgical research can inform acting and directing choices, and how to best rehearse a scene. We will also address the revision process as it applies to the theater process, and introduce some helpful domain-specific terms used in theater that can help your students work together and act together.

Introducing the Play

Throughout this chapter, we will use *The Crucible*, by Arthur Miller as an example of a play that you can approach by reading the entire work or by selecting specific scenes for rehearsal and analysis. As the classroom teacher, you need to decide which approach best serves you and your students. Are you developing a unit that explores Arthur Miller's reaction to McCarthy-era politics through the play? Are you studying the social and political structure that led to the Salem Witch Trials? Are you looking at the playwright's overall intent by tracking how those themes unfold from scene to scene in a play? If so, it would be ideal to read the entire play and use individual scenes to explore the specific objectives and obstacles of different characters. If you have more limited time, if reading is difficult for your students, or if you are mainly interested in bringing life to a text through physicalization, you may want to delve more deeply into several key excerpts. There are more suggestions in Chapter 4 to help you make a decision about how much of the play to explore. If you choose to read the whole play, we recommend doing that after using some of the introductory activities presented in Chapters 3 and 8. You may not have time to for all of the activities, so you can select which of them best serve your students' needs. If you choose to use select scenes or excerpts, you will still need to provide students with enough information about the play to make strong decisions regarding the scenes they will be rehearsing. This information should include a plot summary of the entire play, a character breakdown, themes explored in this play, as well as information about the playwright and his other works. You can keep the information fairly simple, because the scene study activities and strategies will encourage students to be very specific about choices for their characters based on what is happening in the moment of the scene. That is one key difference in how an actor approaches a scene and how a literary critic might. The actor must analyze and play the scene for what is happening in that moment, not what happens in the next scene. The character always lives in the present tense of the scene.

Selecting Scenes and Monologues

When selecting scenes for student work, take a few things into account. Once students are up and on their feet, the main goal is to bring the script to life. If the play contains monologues, consider starting there. You can explore some of the themes of the play through monologue work with the entire class using the group monologue approach described in Chapter 3, then move towards physicalization and character work through scene work in small groups. When choosing scenes, select those written more simply, rather than picking very long and wordy scenes with longer speeches. This allows for students to focus on subtext, physical choices, and possibly memorize the scene quickly. It also makes the reader–feeder exercise we describe later in the chapter work efficiently. You want to pick *high stake* scenes, where the characters have a lot riding on the outcome of the scene. Look for scenes that students can pull apart using the following terms:

Objective: What the characters in the scene want or need. Each character has his/her own objective. State your character's objective with a sentence that begins with "I want to" or "I must."

Obstacle: What is it that stands in the way of getting what you want?

And, finally, pick scenes that will challenge students to incorporate physical movement or *blocking*.

Using *The Crucible* as an example, here are the scenes we selected. We have given you the first line and the last line to indicate where to begin and end the scene as well as a brief synopsis of the action. For the purposes of clarity and diving deep into the text, we've elected not to use the courtroom scenes. You may choose to have students focus on those during a "table read" rather than when they are working in small groups.

Scenes from *The Crucible* (Penguin Edition)

Act I

Scene 1: Abigail and Parris
The central problem in the play is introduced and we learn how high the *stakes* are for Abigail.

Abigail:	Uncle, the rumor of witchcraft is all about.
Abigail:	There is nothin' more, I swear it uncle.

Scene 2: Abigail and the girls
Abigail threatens the girls to cooperate with her, and establishes her *status* as the leader.

Abigail:	How is Ruth sick?
Abigail:	I say shut it, Mary Warren!

Scene 3: Abigail and Proctor
The characters' past relationship is revealed and Abigail makes her *objectives* regarding John very clear.

Proctor:	What's this mischief here?
Abigail:	John, pity me!

Act 2

Scene 4: Hale, Tituba, Parris

Tituba is pressured to confess to conjuring in order to save herself. The *stakes* in the play get higher as she begins to name others.

Hale:	Tituba, I want you to wake this child.
Tituba:	And I look—and there was Goody Good.

Scene 5: Proctor, Elizabeth

Elizabeth and Proctor struggle to connect, Elizabeth's jealousy of Abigail and distrust for John present an *obstacle*.

Proctor:	I think you're sad again. Are you?
Proctor:	Oh, Elizabeth, your justice would freeze beer!

Scene 6: Mary, Elizabeth, Proctor

Elizabeth learns she is accused and Mary Warren asserts her change in *status* in the Proctor home.

Mary:	I made a gift for you today, Goody Proctor.
Elizabeth:	oh, the noose is up!

Scene 7: Proctor, Mary Warren

Proctor pressures Mary Warren to confess the girls' lies. Mary's fear of Abigail *stands in the way*.

Mary:	Mr. Proctor, it is very likely they'll let her come home once they're given proper evidence.
Proctor:	And the wind, God's icy wind, will blow!

Notice that the scenes selected from *The Crucible* are either two-person scenes that allow students to explore the complicated relationships between the play's main characters or three- to four-person scenes that explore Miller's themes regarding hysteria, social pressure, and group-think. You can use similar guidelines to help you make choices about scene selection, and you may also take into account the language demands of the scene, the size of your class, and how many groups you think can work effectively on their own.

When selecting scenes from other plays, you may find that you need to cut some lines or words in order to make a scene more classroom-friendly. For example, Athol Fugard's *"Master Harold" . . . and the boys* contains profanity that you may not want to put in your students' mouths, but the play's conflict and themes merit students reading the play and engaging in classroom scene study. *Master Harold* actually was edited to eliminate profanity when it was published in its entirety in *Scholastic Magazine*. If you consider cutting a scene for language, remember that word choice is critical for a playwright and allowing the profanity in classroom scenework allows for a conversation about the power of words and why that language was chosen. How does it reflect the world of the play or the character's state of mind? This can provide a useful class discussion of when profanity is merely gratuitous and when it can be purposeful or powerful in its application.

Starting the Rehearsal Process

When creating lesson plans involving scene study, a minimum of five class sessions is optimum: two days spent on monologue work, the other three rehearsing and showing selected scenes in small groups. The amount of time you should plan for rehearsal depends on class size, the reading level of your students, and how you showcase the final scenework. If you need to continue work on other required curriculum during this unit, plan to work on your drama project three out of five days per week, or even every other day. The more concentrated the unit, the more quickly your students will retain and build on their newly acquired skills and maintain momentum in their ensemble work. When planning these class periods, continue to include the physical and vocal warm-ups from Chapter 3 that focus the class's energy and concentration as well as turn their attention to character development skills. Here are two additional character-based warm-up activities that take about ten minutes. The discoveries that students make through these exercises can be noted and used later in scenework to make specific intellectual and physical choices for their characters once they have done the basic scene analysis work that we'll introduce shortly.

Activity #1: "Status" Warm-Up

The objective of this exercise is to help students physically explore the idea of status, and how it affects character development. Engage your student actors in a conversation using the following questions:

- ◆ What does status mean to you? At school, at home, or in your wider community?
- ◆ What does status mean on stage? How might it affect the choices you make for your character?

◆ How might a character's status affect their body language? How they use their voice?
◆ How might it affect how they relate to other characters?

You can use this exercise to help provide answers to the questions above. Encourage your students to use what they discover in this exercise to make choices for their characters in their scenework.

To begin this warm-up, four students are each given a slip of paper with a number (1, 2, 3 and 4), which they are to keep as their status number. These students are not to tell anyone else their number and they should not know the numbers of the other members of the group. Students are then given a situation in which the group must make a consensus decision, such as choosing a movie to see or planning the menu for a party. In pursuing the objective, each member of the group maintains the behavior dictated by his or her own status number and tries to determine the status number of the others without asking them directly to reveal it. In playing their status, the numbers work as following:

1. Always in charge.
2. Participates in leadership, but defers to #1. May offer mediation.
3. Offers suggestions, but not leadership, and defers to #1 and #2.
4. May offer suggestions, but always defers to rest of group.

Consider posting this information on a whiteboard or blackboard, so students, both participating and observing, can see it throughout the exercise.

After the scene is played, ask each participant to identify what the status numbers of the others were before divulging their own. Ask audience members if they agree or differ in their perceptions of the status chain of command that they observed.

Activity #2: More "Status" Work

This exercise continues to encourage students to physically and emotionally explore the idea of status. You may want to point out that status can be linked to one's profession or social standing, but that is not always the case. For example, in a scene between a waiter and a world-famous surgeon, the waiter may not always have lower status. Why would that be? Students will need to use their imagination to address that question.

1. Split the class in half. One half of the student actors become the audience and the other half sit in chairs facing the playing area. Using a piece of double-sided tape, place a playing card on each participant's forehead, without allowing the student to see the card.

2. Instruct the actors that an "ace" is the highest status in the room and a "two" is the lowest. When the facilitator claps his/her hands, the actors are to mill around the room as if they are at a social engagement, meeting new people for the first time. They are to treat the other people at the party according to the status (card ranking) on their forehead. They are to quickly adapt their character by responding to the cues given to them by their fellow actors.
3. The first round is silent and entirely delivered through body language and facial expression. Once students have moved through space reacting to the other participants based on their status number, call out "Freeze" to end the round.
4. Clap again and the second round introduces improvised dialogue that would reflect their reaction to the other participants' status. Allow participants once again to interact. Then call out "Freeze."
5. The actors sit back down in their seats and are asked to sit right to left from low to high status, having to guess what external status they have been given. One at a time actors remove their cards and discuss if their predictions were correct, how they guessed their status, how they were treated, and how it felt.

These status exercises work best when you have built a trusting ensemble. As students explore how it feels to play different statuses, vulnerability is required and uncomfortable feelings may arise. This is all part of the creative risk-taking we discussed in Chapter 3. We recommend following this activity with a conversation about the status of different characters in the play, and in the specific scenes your students are rehearsing.

Katherine McKnight and Mary Scrugg's book, *The Second City Guide to Improv in the Classroom: Using Improvisation to Teach Skills and Improve Learning* (Jossey-Bass, 2008), offers variations on these status activities as well as other character-focused activities to expand a class's personal warm-up toolkit.

More Body and Character Connections

Getting up in front of a class to perform a scene or monologue can be intimidating, and students may get very nervous. If you give them some specific direction regarding how to explore a character physically, they will be less self-conscious and may even be able to conquer some nervous actions that can happen when you get in front of a group like stepping side to side or swaying. Actors who approach their work in a very physical way will typically take a lot of time deciding where the character they are playing "lives" in his or her body. The four most common areas are: *head*, *heart*, *belly*, and *pelvis*. Have a conversation with students about what that choice might mean for how their character moves and approaches life.

Activity #3: Making the Connection

Step 1: Ask students to generate a list of five celebrities and what part of their body leads them. You might ask willing students to demonstrate how those celebrities move.

Step 2: Have students draw from a hat a slip with one of the four body centers. Then instruct them move around the room inhabiting that area of their body.

Step 3: Debrief the experience by asking students the following questions:

- o How does it affect how they feel?
- o How they interact with others?

This activity will help students make some differentiations between themselves and the character they are exploring, especially if the character seems very different from the student portraying him/her. As with all acting, the students' own individuality will also dictate character choice. Activities like an opinionaire, the human barometer, and gallery walks discussed in Chapters 6 and 8 will focus more on their immediate personal connection with a character.

The combination of emotional exploration and physical work used in the exercises above should create a basic toolbox that students can pull from as they begin to work on scenes together. They know they can and should use their own feelings and connection to what is happening in the play, they know that they can transform their posture and tone to reflect the status of their character in relation to others in the scene, and they can think about where the character lives in their body in order to be less self-conscious and to make specific physical choices about how their character moves through the world of the play.

Casting the Scenes, Creating Rehearsal Groups

In many ways, a scene involving two characters is ideal. Students can concentrate on the relationship between those two characters: the stakes present in the scene, the characters' individual and/or common objectives, and the obstacles faced by each character to achieve their objective. We will be focusing shortly on how to work a two-character scene in groups of four, but first you need to address the rehearsal groups. We tend to let students self-select their groups, using the following criteria, "Pick a group of four that you feel you can work well with, focus with, and take creative risks with." Naturally, there will be student combinations that you may have reservations about. You may have to separate individuals with antagonistic relationships or who have a hard time focusing together on the task at hand with their best friends. But, in general, students tend to make good choices, and we think you'll see that your pre-rehearsal ensemble building activities will translate to the group work. You may even be surprised and delighted by some of the combinations of students who work well together.

When selecting parts and assigning each group a scene, encourage your students to pick whichever part interests them most, regardless of gender. Our work is process based, not based on the expectations of an audience. It would take too much time if we tried to cast every scene as it might be cast in a professional theater. And non-traditional casting provides students with the opportunity to explore what it is like to stand in another's shoes, whether they are the same gender or not. If you run into instances where a student is reluctant to play another gender, you can make adjustments to the group, or swap that student into another group, but we have very rarely run into that problem. Students tend to understand the purpose of the rehearsal process and what we are trying to get out of it. You will want to encourage them to make honest and truthful choices for their characters whether they are playing their own gender or not. Yes, you may get some campy choices at first. That is OK. Once you challenge students to commit to the objectives, obstacles, and stakes in the scene, and to find their personal connection to the character, whether that be a man or a woman, gender probably will not be the most important element about their character.

Starting with a "Table Read"

With most productions, the first rehearsal involves the director and actors sitting around a table to read the entire script. If you are choosing to tackle the entire script or excerpted scenes, we suggest imitating this approach. Attention is paid to understand the words on the page: how they are properly pronounced, what they mean, and how they reveal what the character is thinking as well as how they are behaving onstage. Usually the production's assistant director or stage manager reads aloud any of the stage directions provided by the playwright or included by the initial production's prompt script. Beginning any rehearsal process with this approach requires very close reading of the text, and it usually takes a professional cast several days.

Once students have been "cast" into their scenework ensembles, they should read their scene aloud in a table read to make sure that they understand what the characters are saying and doing, and if they don't, perform on-the-spot research using a dictionary and/or an online search engine. They also can consult any of the dramaturgical material, or background information, you have provided or students have researched themselves. In addition to unfamiliar words, students should be alert for references to people, places, things, and customs relating to the play's time and place. For example, *The Crucible* draws on events surrounding the Salem Witch Trials, so the character's use of archaic pronouns, such as "thee" and "thou" or means of address like "Goody" makes better sense when placed in their historical and religious context. Chapter 6 will address introducing the role of the dramaturg into this process and when students might conduct certain types of research to support their understanding of the script and the world it creates.

Students should annotate their scripts documenting the information they have gained to understand the words themselves as well as note questions they have about characters' motivation, the connection of their isolated scene to the entire play, and the time period of the conflict. If they have experience annotating a novel, transferring that skill to the work of an actor should not seem foreign at all.

The time allocated for a table read might be limited to half a class period or more depending on how much on-the-spot research students must conduct to make good sense of the text. Since they will take on the role of either a reader–feeder or an actor once the scene is up on its feet, have the reader–feeder and the actor take turns reading the script to encourage not only close reading but close listening as well. The more students understand what they are saying and read it aloud with authority, the more fruitful the rehearsal process, so give students enough "table time" before getting them on their feet.

The Reader–Feeder Approach

We use a process we call "reader–feeder" to rehearse scenes in groups. You may find similar rehearsal techniques inspired by famed acting teacher Constantin Stanislavky, who didn't want his actors tied to their scripts during rehearsal. Tina Packer and Shakespeare and Company call their variation "feeding in." Similar to these rehearsal strategies, our reader–feeder technique liberates students from constantly looking down at their script and allows them to focus on eye contact and physical movement. This approach requires very sophisticated teamwork on the part of everyone in the group, and it encourages the full participation of all members, including students who are more shy and don't want to be the focus of a scene. As a "reader–feeder", those students are still very much part of the group, but out of the spotlight. It also helps aural learners memorize lines more quickly, if memorization is a goal for your class.

Here is how the reader–feeder approach works:

1. Divide students into groups of four or six, and give each group a two- or three-character scene. Designate two students as the "actors" in the group, and two students as the "reader–feeders." One actor and one reader are assigned for each character in the scene and work as a pair to read that part.

2. The readers stand close to the actors and hold the script. The readers read the lines to each actor as if though through an earpiece and the actors repeat the lines, adding feeling, emotion, action, and gesture. Students need time to work as a team and negotiate how to best work together in this foursome.

3. Readers will need to learn how to break up lines so that the actor can comprehend them, and they will need to adjust their volume so that their actor can hear them. The actors need to trust their readers to give them the information they need and to take creative risks as they explore the scene vocally and physically.

4. As the groups become comfortable with this way of working, they can begin to direct themselves, especially adding meaningful movement using the acting space effectively. This process requires sophisticated teamwork and sensitivity, and showcases ensemble work beautifully once students master the technique.

Side-coaching suggestion to apply revision process to rehearsal:

Ultimately, the rehearsal process should become dynamic, not simply repetitive. At first, students may think they are "done" after they have run through a scene a couple of times. Challenge them to constantly develop the scene, and to make new choices. In this way, students are adopting the revision process mindset to their performance work. They are applying critical thinking to develop attentiveness to subtleties and distinctions as they make interpretative choices, and find better insights into the characters' stories.

Side-coaching suggestions to encourage critical thinking in rehearsal:

You can spend some time with each group, prompting them with questions that help them explore the scene more deeply, such as:

○   What is happening in the play at this point?
○   What is happening in the scene?
○   What is the character's objective in this scene?
○   What is the character's obstacle?
○   How can blocking help tell the story?

Once you feel that the groups have intellectually grasped what is happening in the scene, it's time to move the work off the page and onto the stage. Students can effectively perform their scenes using the reader–feeder technique without necessarily memorizing the script, which keeps the reader–feeder involved in sharing the scene with the class. It is surprising how the feeder and the actor become one in a well-rehearsed scene.

Moving with a Purpose: Blocking the Scene

Blocking is the term used in theater to describe the movement in a scene. An example of blocking would be "Character A crosses to the door, looks through the peephole, then quickly hides behind a chair." It can be as simple as, "Character B turns her back on Character A." Blocking is used to either help tell the story (we think the character is in danger because he hides behind a chair), or to develop characterization (Character B never sits in the presence of anyone). The only rules we would suggest include:

◆   Never make a classmate feel unsafe with your blocking choices.
◆   For the purposes of a classroom showing, don't turn your back to the audience.
◆   Don't upstage your fellow actor by forcing them to turn their back to the audience in order to talk to you.

Blocking is one way to show different interpretations of the same scene, and for the amount of time you will be spending on these scenes, we'll reiterate that there are no wrong choices—only choices. As your students continue to rehearse and revise the scene, they may change their blocking. Similar to the Sound Around activity from Chapter 3, suggest strong gestures and movements rather than small, tentative ones. Have a conversation about the difference between film acting, where actors can make very small and subtle movements, expressions, and gestures because a camera can zoom in, and the stage, where an actor needs to be able to transmit emotion through voice and moment to the back row of a theater. With all of these activities, encourage creative risk-taking as students begin to block their scenes. They can always tone a scene down later.

If groups have an uneven number of students, if the class is very large, or if certain students are suited to leadership roles, assign a director for each scene. Otherwise, let each group discover how they want to portray characters' objectives and their relationships through simple, strong movements. We like to challenge each group to find at least three apparent and appropriate blocking choices per scene.

Showing Scenes

Through all of these activities, the focus is on process, rather than product. But, it's still a lot of fun to share all of the hard work, risk-taking, and creativity applied to the rehearsal process with some scene showings for the whole class. It also gives students an opportunity to practice being a good audience.

As audience members, encourage your students to:

◆ Bring focused energy.
◆ Be supportive.
◆ Be engaged.
◆ Encourage feedback by asking the audience to share something that worked well and suggest something that should be expanded.

As performers, encourage your students to:

◆ Trust their reader–feeder ensemble.
◆ Bring focused energy.
◆ Project their voices.
◆ Persevere if they get the giggles or lose focus in other ways.

In our experience, final scene showings give students immediate positive reinforcement for making bold choices, staying focused, and living in the moment of the scene. Students' strengths and weaknesses will be revealed in a way that few other activities can expose. How you choose to provide feedback and to reward participation is up to you, but in the next section we'll present some ways to measure your students' growth.

Assessment: What Are My Students Learning? How Do They Want to Grow?

Assessing arts-based learning is always somewhat subjective. Rehearsing and showing scenes requires different criteria from most activities in an ELA classroom. Because this process will be very different for each student and each student will encounter different challenges, self-assessment is a powerful tool. It will help you understand where students are starting this process and where they hope to see themselves going. Students should assess themselves on areas such as self-expression, confidence, projection, or teamwork.

You will find an example of a basic self-assessment tool at the end of the chapter that requires to students to select several behavioral goals (Handout 5.1). At the end of a rehearsal/performance process, students would provide observable, anecdotal evidence to illustrate how well they met specific goals.

Obviously, the rehearsal process we introduce through this chapter is abbreviated. It truncates the long, complicated journey that an actor takes from the time he/she attends her first rehearsal to an opening night performance. Our goal here is to integrate the theatre arts into your classroom practice and show you how the tools an actor employs can help students unpack a text and bring it to life in a meaningful way. The main focuses of our classroom pedagogy are ensemble building, simple, but effective text analysis and developing actor skills that students should be able to transfer to other areas of learning. As you think about assessing the work your students do, you will need to set expectations that are appropriate to the class you are working with.

As students rehearse the scenes you've chosen, you are challenging them to work in an ensemble to the best of that group's ability, but you are also asking students to do some very personal work on character development. To keep students mindful of all the elements that go into a strong scene showing, you may want to share a simple checklist with each group that outlines your expectations at this point in their work. We include such a checklist at the end of the chapter (Handout 5.2). You can adapt it as appropriate.

We also include a rubric for scene work that can be used as you spend time with each group during class time (Handout 5.3). You can also ask each group to self-assess their own work as an ensemble with this same tool. The rubric gives students three rounds for revision and each round has a progressively sophisticated objective. You will be measuring growth in three areas: work as an ensemble, text analysis, and then interpretation of that text through blocking and character choices. You may choose to use this tool as a summative assessment, with round 3 being the final scene showing to the classroom.

Building Confidence, Fostering Success

Assessing arts-based activities can tilt towards the subjective, but we've focused on a number of theater-specific skills that you should be able to assess using whichever model works best for your purposes. We've shared some domain-specific terms (blocking, objective, obstacle, stakes), and we've explored how to teach skills like projection, articulation, and text analysis for the actor. Students become more confident and more comfortable expressing themselves through these activities and that growth can and will translate to other areas of your students' academic success.

Opportunity for Reflection

Consider how you might apply ideas from this chapter to your own classroom.

1. How does close reading help unlock the themes and character development in an immediate way when you are studying a script?
2. Do you see increased engagement when you increase physicality in your curriculum? If your students are enjoying this process, do you see a link between student interest and engagement and improved close reading skills?
3. Does this process help students learn how to give and receive constructive criticism during a scene showing? Can this skill set be used throughout the year?
4. How do the skills learned in this unit transfer to other areas of student learning?

Handout 5.1: Self-Assessment: My Personal Goals

Name:_____

In this project, you will be accountable to your ensemble, but please also think about being accountable to yourself. What goals do you have for your own work on this project? Set one personal goal that will help you improve a specific performance behavior.

For example:

- ◆ I will challenge myself to stay focused and not laugh while performing in front of others.
- ◆ I will be able to express my creative ideas about blocking to my rehearsal group.
- ◆ I will memorize my lines (if that is an expectation).

Primary goal: _____

Why did you select this as primary behavior you would like to improve?

How will improving this behavior help you support your scenework ensemble members?

At the end of the rehearsal/performance cycle: What evidence can you provide that demonstrates you have improved in any way in this area?

Secondary goal (optional): _____

Why do want to include this goal in addition to your primary focus?

At the end of the rehearsal/performance cycle: What evidence can you provide that demonstrates you have improved in any way in this area?

Handout 5.2: Formative Assessment: Checklist for Meeting Rehearsal Objectives

Ensemble Building

_____Students fully engaged with ensemble. They are keeping each other on task.

_____Together they are making strong choices, suggestions for revision and redirecting focus and energy when needed.

_____All members of the ensemble have the opportunity to be a reader and an actor.

Scene Work Specifics

_____Each character in this scene has a clear, observable **objective** that he/she is pursuing.

_____The time and place of this scene is clear to the actors and the audience/observer.

_____Their scene has at least three clear **blocking** choices that help tell the story.

Character Work

_____Students have explored the **status** of each character in the scene.

_____The relationship between the characters in the scene is clear.

_____Students have taken some creative risks in exploring the choices of their characters.

Actor Skills

_____Students are projecting their voices and articulating their words so that the audience can understand them.

_____Students are focused on their scene partner(s) and their reader–feeder partner.

_____The reader–feeder process is working toward fluid, seamless integration and does not disrupt rhythm or meaning of the dialogue.

_____Students integrate movement suitable to their characters and minimize distracting behaviors not consistent with a character and his/her circumstances.

Additional suggestions to explore during next phase of rehearsal process:

Handout 5.3: Rubric: Assessment for Research Process and Final Scene Showings

Ensemble members:

Round 1: Ensemble Work: Students negotiate how to work as a team and make sense of the "reader–feeder" exercise

1	2	3	4
Students struggle and abandon the effort to work as a team			Students successfully negotiate and make sense of the exercise

Notes:

Round 2: Close Reading/Textual comprehension: Teams make sense of playwright's intention and storytelling for the scene

1	2	3	4
Students struggle to comprehend the text of the scene and how it relates to the play as a whole			Students engaged, effectively working on textual problem solving, understanding the scene within the context of the play

Notes:

Round 3: Revision: Students begin to make inferential and improvisational decisions about the scene taking creative risks and exploring different choices for their characters

1	2	3	4
Scene does not develop significantly from first read through			Significant and observable progress made during the rehearsal process

Notes:

6

Discovering the World of the Play: Researching Complementary Non-Fiction, Primary Sources, and Visual Texts

If the goal of performing scenes and speeches is to help students step into the shoes of their characters then conducting appropriate research to better understand the time and place those characters inhabit will help students know how to wear those shoes with authority. With that said, those student-performers can take on another role critical to any theatrical production, the dramaturg. This chapter will define the role of a professional dramaturg and how both teachers and their students can conduct useful, collaborative, shareable research when they take on that role.

Reading a play does not require the same amount of time and effort as reading a novel. Students studying a play that addresses a social issue or historical event can benefit from reading or viewing non-fiction, primary sources, and visual texts to better understand the work's overall context. Those non-fiction texts and primary sources can provide challenging reading experiences. Applying the appropriate reading strategies offered in Chapters 4 and 7 and allowing students to locate, select, and edit contextual resources will make those texts more accessible and meaningful to the play reading and scene rehearsals.

What Is a Dramaturg?

A dramaturg is a member of a theater production team who researches and prepares the materials directors, actors, and designers need to fully understand the text and context of a play. They study the play carefully to provide insights about the author's work and they share these with the cast. They also serve as in-house critic, providing feedback to the director and actors during rehearsal, especially for the production of new plays. They often create materials for the audience and work closely with education departments to prepare materials for students and teachers.

When assigned to a particular production, the dramaturg reads through the script to determine the typical and unique types of information required by the director, designers, and actors. For example, Bruce Norris' play *Clybourne Park* is set in two different eras in the same setting, a house in Chicago. The first act is set in 1959 and the second act in 2009. The play is related to Lorraine Hansberry's *A Raisin in the Sun*, since the action in both acts takes place in the house that the Younger family purchased. In the first act Karl Linder, a minor character in Hansberry's play, tries convince the white homeowners to back out of the impending sale to a black family. The second act is set in that same house 50 years later as relatives of the Youngers plan to sell it to a white family as the all-black neighborhood begins to gentrify. To prepare background information for *Clybourne Park*, the dramaturg would research information on the playwright, the Pulitzer Prize winning play's production history, its connections to another acclaimed play, controversial real estate practices in the Chicago area, and the sociological impact of changing demographics in neighborhoods on Chicago's south side from the 1959 to 2009. The research would then be formatted into a booklet, packet, or webpage, which the dramaturg would share during the preproduction phase and the rehearsal process. The dramaturg would continue to supplement that information at any point during rehearsals based on requests made by the director, designers, or actors.

The task of the professional dramaturg can be transformed effectively into a collaborative effort which includes the efforts of an entire class. Small groups would be assigned segments of the overall task: locating information from a variety of print and online sources, evaluating those sources, selecting appropriate information, writing summaries, formatting information, and creating a shareable final product. The duties of the dramaturg can also be assumed by the teacher based on the goals of a unit that integrates the study of an entire play or select scenes.

Teacher as Dramaturg: Providing Students with Complementary Non-Fiction Texts

The teacher can assume the role of dramaturg by selecting non-fiction reading and viewing experiences to provide students with a play's necessary background and context. An online search will yield existing dramaturgical packets adapted for audience members or as a teacher handbook. Those online dramaturgical materials provide a professional example to model or a ready-made range of sources for immediate selection. When TimeLine Theatre produced *A Raisin in the Sun*, dramaturg Alexis Jade Links organized her research into three segments: History of the Play, The Given Circumstances, Suggested Readings/Modern Contexts. That format can guide the selection of three meaningful reading experiences to frame a classroom study of the play.

Tackling the "history of the play" certainly should include information about the author as well the play's production history and cultural legacy. In the first section Links also includes an essay by Jacob Shuler called "Dream on a Make-Down Bed: Tenement Life from the Great Migration to the 1950s" and a piece from *Chicago Magazine* (March 2013) by Dan Rubin titled "What is 'gentrification'?"

To address "the given circumstances of the play," Links provides a "History of Nigeria" to help contextualize Beneatha's interest in the Pan-African Movement. Links adapts information from the Library of Congress, but that source could be easily replaced with a similar overview of pertinent Nigerian history from any number of online sources that fit more appropriately with students' reading level.

Two selections from Links' final section of suggested readings can pair Booker T. Washington's inspirational and optimisitic "Cast Down Your Bucket" speech from 1895 with an excerpt from Ariel Prince's book *The Robert Taylor Homes Failure of Public Housing* that critically argues how the "built for efficiency" mentality of Chicago's public housing initiative from the 1940s through the 1960s was no better than life on a crowded slave ship.

As print texts are considered and selected, a dramaturg also suggests visual and video texts, which supports appealing to different learning styles in a student population. A quick online search will yield a number of short YouTube videos of interviews with Lorraine Hansberry or the play being discussed by scholars or theater directors. The Radical Cartography website offers maps that track the race and ethnic demographics of Chicago neighborhoods in 2000 and 2010. Ronit Bezalel's two films *Voices of Cabrini* (1999), a 30-minute documentary about the demolition of that housing project, and *70*

Acres in Chicago: Cabrini Green (2015), a 63-minute follow-up, vividly address the challenges of displacing a public housing residents and the challenges of new mixed income housing on the former project's site.

The selection of these supplemental texts should be guided by what students already know about the historical and cultural context of the world of the play, so teachers should administer an anticipatory set of questions or activities to measure their prior knowledge. Crafting an "opinionaire" like the one included in Chapter 8 can provide a quick and easy measure of what students can bring from their other literature and social studies experiences. Dramaturgical reading and viewing do not have to be "front loaded" before reading or rehearsing the play. Since some of the reading selections are more challenging, it would be best to pace those activities before, during, and after the reading and rehearsal process. And as curriculum design should respond to students' different reading abilities and need for information, students might be allowed to choose teacher-selected materials to read or view at specific stages in the play reading and rehearsal process to foster greater ownership of that information. Formative and summative activities presented in Chapter 8 can draw on that dramaturgical informative to assess students' level of understanding and appropriate application of that information.

Students as Dramaturgs: Researching the World of the Play

Assuming the role of the dramaturg will give students the opportunity to conduct authentic research to augment and enhance their understanding of the play regardless whether they are exploring key scenes and monologues or studying the play in full.

Athol Fugard's play *"Master Harold" and . . . the boys* will serve as a model text for building dramaturgical resources collaboratively. The play is based on Fugard's experiences growing up in South Africa under the apartheid system. The action takes place on a single afternoon when a white teenager, Harold, or "Hally" as he is called in the play, returns after school to his parents' tearoom in Port Elizabeth, South Africa in 1950 where two black adult employees are tending the business. A series of phone calls reveals that Hally's chronically ill father has been hospitalized. The play's conflict surrounds Hally struggling to resist his father's influence on both personal and societal levels, while reconciling the profound effect that one of those black employees, Sam, who has acted as a father figure since Hally's childhood, has had on him.

When TimeLine Theatre mounted a production of the play, dramaturg Kelli Marino created a packet of materials for the director, actors, and design team that covered the following topics:

◆ the playwright's biography;
◆ the plays of Athol Fugard;
◆ Fugard's awards and nominations;
◆ direct quotations of statements Fugard has made on theater and his career;
◆ the production history of the play;
◆ the intersection of the play's action and Fugard's own life;
◆ information about the history and culture of South Africa in the 1950s:

  ○ apartheid;
  ○ timeline of significant events in apartheid in South Africa;
  ○ Port Elizabeth in the 1950s (setting of the play);
  ○ St. George Park (an important place discussed by characters in the play);
  ○ ballroom dance in South Africa;
  ○ jazz music in South Africa;

◆ terms found in the script that require definition or explanation.

Students can easily divide up the research tasks to assemble this kind of information. Handout 6.1 at the end of this chapter will help students brainstorm ideas for research. Some of those suggestions can be explored before students even begin to read the play. For example, they know who wrote the play, so the first five items on the list would constitute the pre-reading research activities. Since the students can, and should, know that the play is set in South Africa in the 1950s, gathering information about the apartheid system and creating a timeline could easily be accomplished as pre-reading research. If students are reading the play in full, researching the autobiographical elements of the play as well as information about Port Elizabeth, St. George Park, ballroom dance, and jazz music would be better investigated once the students have begun to read the script or rehearse their scenes. In that way their work is slightly different from the work of the dramaturg, since the research is not fully conducted prior to beginning of a reading or rehearsal process.

As students assume specific research responsibilities, they need to be instructed or reminded about the merits and perils of surfing the web for reliable information: Which websites have the most reliable information and which don't? They also need to brush up on summary skills and citing information that is directly lifted or quoted from an Internet source. Dramaturgical packets can involve useful "cutting and pasting" of primary source excerpts, and those pieces of text need careful source documentation. For example in the *"Master Harold" . . . and the boys* packet, the dramaturg includes a reference list of 32 citations, including both print and online sources. The information gleaned from this research process will need a shareable format and an online platform might involve contributions to Google Drive or a class wiki. Assuming the role of the dramaturg gives the research meaning and value. The acquisition process is owned by the class as a whole and informs everyone's greater understanding of the world of the play through direct investigative experience.

The "Terms to Know" feature of the dramaturgy is probably the most valuable aspect to students' close reading process. Using any available classroom or personal technology, the list of terms can be built as students read. Establishing a Google Drive or wiki for this feature will enable students to contribute to that list with the term and a citation for the definition or explanation. In *Master Harold*, there is challenging vocabulary (i.e. intrepid, scalars, flotsam, jetsam, deportment), "British English" and Afrikaans words and idioms (i.e. sixpence, nought, donner), outdated slang (i.e. donkey's years, brained), music and dance terminology (quickstep, foxtrot, Sarah Vaughan), and references to South African culture, geography, or history (Basuto, Standard 9, Transvaal, General Smuts). The task of creating a collaborative list of terms and definitions can be accomplished whether students are reading the play for homework or reading the play aloud in class as a table read. If students are reading the play aloud, one of the students could be assigned as the "dramaturg of the day" to stop the reading at the end of a speech or conversation to highlight a term that clearly needs some on-the-spot defining or to poll the class if there are any words or concepts they found confusing.

If a group of students might not be able to assume the task of identifying and defining appropriate terms easily or effectively, the teacher might set up a "basic list" of terms with the understanding that students can add terms and their definitions to that list as well.

Seeing the World of the Play Through Visual Media Research

A playwright can bring actors and their audience into a world that has been documented extensively by photographers and filmmakers. As mentioned earlier, dramaturgs do not limit the information they gather to print texts. As students assume the role of the dramaturg, they can conduct a search for visual texts.

Many times it is important for directors, actors, and designers to see the world of the play as it existed or still exists to inform a production's "look". When TimeLine Theatre's dramaturg, Josh Altman, compiled information for Aaron Posner's dramatization of *My Name Is Asher Lev*, based on Chaim

Potok's novel set in the Hasidic community in Brooklyn from the 1950s, he included a gallery of photos for actors' and designers' reference. Since Asher Lev is an artist, there are references to specific works of art in the dialogue including Marc Chagall's *White Cross*, so the packet provided images of paintings and sculpture. For the production of Michelle Lowe's play *Inana*, which focuses on the recovery and preservation of ancient archaeological artifacts after the 2003 looting of the Mosul Museum in Iraq, Maren Robinson's dramaturgical packet included a wide range of pictoral information: maps, diagrams, photos of the archaeological artifacts and the looter's destruction of museum displays.

Photos included in most dramaturgical packets typically are posted in the rehearsal room to keep those visual reference points in sight. Even though active approaches to scene study don't require costume or set design and execution, posting collected photos in the classroom promotes a more immersive experience for students and can become a part of a more extensive and formalized gallery of materials that mimics a theater lobby display.

In addition to photographs, art reproductions, maps, diagrams, charts, and graphs, helpful visual material also should include any pertinent media texts. Compiling video links for a production of *The Laramie Project* would include locally and nationally broadcast news clips that covered the discovery of Matthew Shepard's body, the investigation of the crime, and the prosecution of his murderers; a subject-specific documentary, *Matthew Shepard Is A Friend of Mine*; a documentary with a broader perspective on hate crimes, *Not In Our Town*; and a documentary on the roots of gay rights and activism, *Stonewall Uprising*. These video resources provide a glimpse into the specific events and the broader social context that became the raw materials for the play's script.

The Play's "Backstory": Creating a Dramaturgical Packet

Once students have conducted their research, the next step involves compiling that information into an edited, shareable form. Most dramaturgs will present their research in booklet or packet form, sometimes called the "actor's bible." At TimeLine Theatre that dramaturgical material is formatted into a study guide for teachers and students who participate in Living History school residencies as well as another version for audience members. Subscribers also receive a "Backstory" for each production through the mail or online. It is a multi-page preview of a play that provides pertinent information about the play, the playwright, and its historical, social or political contexts.

A dramaturgical packet isn't simply a bibliography of print and online sources. It isn't just cutting and pasting text gleaned from those sources. A dramaturg needs to summarize, analyze, and synthesize information, so those initial research activities inevitably lead to practical writing activities that reinforce students' ability to paraphrase or reformat information responsibly and to cite the sources of that information appropriately. When students assemble their information, they can use Alexis Jade Link's packet for *Raisin in the Sun* an exemplar. Again, she chooses to divide her research into three categories: History of the Play, Given Circumstances, Suggested Reading and Viewing.

Students also can design, write, and publish their own version of a "Backstory" for the play that they are studying and performing. This task would require students to pare down the information provided to the actors by considering what is essential for an audience member to know prior to attending a performance. Dividing the labor among all the class members is very easy. First of all, the class would decide which of the following elements typically found in TimeLine's publication would be included in their "Backstory":

- ◆ Cover art: a graphic design that visually projects the content, mood, and/or theme of the play, as well as including the theater's logo, the title of the play, and its author.
- ◆ A "message": the theater's artistic director writes about the selection of the play and how it fits into the theater overall mission or that particular season of plays.
- ◆ The play and playwright—and possibly source material for plays adapted from existing material like a novel, memoir, journalistic reporting, etc.
- ◆ The timeline of relevant historical events, movements, or watershed moments related to the play.
- ◆ Words and their definitions: a selection of words, concepts, allusions to historical figures, literature or pop culture that are most important for the audience's understanding of the characters and conflict.
- ◆ "The interview" or "the collaboration": focus on the director, an actor, a designer or a combination of several contributors to the production's development.
- ◆ Photographs and other images:

    ○ archival images of pertinent historical figures, places, or events;
    ○ rehearsal photos;
    ○ head shots of the author, pertinent production staff members.

Pdf files of "Backstory" editions for the following plays can be found online:

My Name Is Asher Lev: http://www.timelinetheatre.com/asher_lev/ TimeLine_MyNameIsAsherLev_Backstory.pdf

A Raisin in the Sun: http://www.timelinetheatre.com/raisin_in_the_ sun/TimeLine_RaisinInTheSun_Backstory.pdf

Inana: http://www.timelinetheatre.com/inana/TimeLine_Inana_ Backstory.pdf

The Normal Heart: http://www.timelinetheatre.com/normal_heart/ TimeLine_NormalHeart_Backstory.pdf

A class-produced "Backstory" can be easily shared with parents on a classroom website, especially if the play being studied addresses a particularly timely issue or event. For example, John Conroy's *My Kind of Town*, a play about police torture and department corruption, had increasing relevance not only in Chicago where the action is set but as the Black Lives Matter movement gained momentum in the wake of police shootings across the country beginning in Ferguson, Missouri in 2014. A reading of the play was staged as a community event at a Chicago public high school, and the publication of a student produced "Backstory" would nicely complement that outreach initiative for audience members who did not attend the full stage production at TimeLine Theatre.

Step into the Play's World: Creating a "Lobby Display" for the Classroom

Finally, a dramaturg usually collaborates with the artistic staff to assemble an extensive lobby display that further reformats pertinent research for the audience's quick consumption. Since TimeLine Theatre's mission focuses on engaging audiences in plays that address significant historical figures, issues, and events, informative and interactive lobby displays have been a hallmark of the theater experience. For their production of *A Raisin in the Sun*, audience members walked through a hallway evocative of the one found in the Younger family's apartment building. The display featured information regarding the author, the real estate industry's redlining practices in Chicago, and other racial and ethnic segregation norms of the 1950s. An enlargement of Langston Hughes' poem "Harlem" formed an interactive focal point of that production's lobby display. Audience members were asked to answer the question,

"What becomes of a dream deferred?" and to pin their response to the space around the poem. For Michelle Lowe's play *Inana*, the lobby display provided photographs of important cultural artifacts and works of art spanning human history and similarly asked audience members to place a stick pin next to the item that they would save, which parallels the play's protagonist struggle to preserve the ancient statue of the goddess Inana. Students can adapt key information once again from the original dramaturgical research as well as decide on an appropriate interactive feature to create a "lobby display" on a classroom wall or bulletin.

The research activities presented in this chapter cover the gamut of what a dramaturg, or student-researchers, can tackle while investigating the world of any play. In their classroom application, it is impractical to consider embarking on all of these tasks and their resulting products. The reasons why a play is selected, which companion texts it supports, and where it fits in a given unit will guide what serves students and their learning goals best. As mentioned before, the research and viewing materials students assemble and experience as they read, discuss, and rehearse a play lay the foundation for a variety of writing, speaking, and media production covered in Chapter 8 that lead to both formative and summative assessments. The research skills developed, refined, or supported through dramaturgical investigation also transfer to other more traditional research projects and products.

Opportunity for Reflection

Consider how you might apply ideas from this chapter to your own classroom.

1. How does dramaturgical information gathering meet the existing curricular objectives for honing research skills?
2. How does the dramaturgical information gathering parallel and support the process involved in a traditional research paper?
3. How does creating a dramaturgical packet, a "Backstory" publication, and a classroom display help students understand how the same pool of information can be tailored for different purposes, formats, and audiences?
4. How does introducing the role of a dramaturg encourage students to be more curious about the elements of a play, or any work of art that moves them? Is curiosity a skill that you are trying to cultivate with your students?

Handout 6.1: Brainstorming to Set a Research Agenda

Name of play:

Quickly skim the information that the publisher provides on the front and back cover of your edition of the play as well as a Wikipedia entry on the play. You want to brainstorm possibilities for research tasks when you and your classmates take on the role of dramaturg.

Playwright's life and career:

Time period of play:

Themes presented in play:

Issues or events addressed in play:

Images, artwork or media texts to help visualize the world of the play:

It's All Connected: Making Interdisciplinary Connections Through Dramatic Texts

Using dramatic literature in Social Studies classrooms as a springboard for exploring an historical event or unpacking a social issue might not be a common practice or seem a natural fit for the curriculum. This chapter will provide examples of how the study of dramatic literature can enrich existing curricula in Social Studies and interdisciplinary American Studies classrooms.

Why Make Interdisciplinary Connections Through Dramatic Texts?

In Chapter 4, "The Play's the Thing," we identified what makes a better reader, and we suggested strong reading strategies to help all readers improve. We stressed the skill of reading, and we stressed the way reading a play is different from reading non-fiction or other genres of fiction. In this chapter, we would like to dig more deeply into the critical-thinking skills that develop on an interdisciplinary level when plays are built into the Social Studies classroom. As we have said, plays bring history to life, shed light on a historical topic, provide a narrative or counter-narrative to history, and create opportunities for rich, more sophisticated thinking experiences for students. Building these interdisciplinary connections between fiction and non-fiction creates contexts for learning that open other rigorous and engaging experiences for our students.

Pairing a history play with the study of history as non-fiction opens up many avenues for higher-level, interdisciplinary thinking—where students need to compare and contrast, make judgments, evaluate, apply, and create an argument with dimension.

Before we get started, let's tackle the long-standing concern of teaching a Social Studies class, which sounds something like: "There is so much content we need to cover! When can a teacher ever spend the time reading a play on top of everything else? The curriculum tells me I need to cover three thousand years of history! How am I to add one more thing?" That is a legitimate point.

But changes in education demand a shift away from curriculum that spans volumes of content. Think: "Less is more." Better educators are addressing the challenge of developing higher-order, critical-thinking skills instead of dumping content in front of students. These educators recognize that less content and deeper analysis leads to more engaged learning and greater thinking opportunities. Working out the relationship between historical non-fiction and historical fiction helps to enrich the critical-thinking capacity and the engagement of students.

Please, remember, students do not need to read the *entire* play in order to gain greater perspective or insight. As we have explored in Chapter 5, you can work with excerpts from a play and summarize the story around the excerpt. Find a key scene or a monologue that expresses the central conflict within the historical figure or event. Allow a small piece of a play to stand on its own. Use the excerpt as a way to launch into a discussion of history or to explore another way of viewing history thematically. We will cover that more in this chapter.

With every passing day there is more history to cover. By educating students with more interdisciplinary experiences, let's take on the challenge of how we approach the study of history in a way that develops skillful thinking. That effort will mean revisiting curriculum choices and making smarter decisions about how to instruct Social Studies. That might seem like a big challenge, but this chapter encourages us to start small and find other in-roads to engage the fiction and non-fiction interdisciplinary relationship. As we all continue to improve our instructional approaches, more inventive ideas will develop. Consider these suggestions a good starting point for your own ideas.

Excerpting a Play, Capturing a Crucial Moment in History

As we noted, reading an entire play is not necessary. In much of the work we do, we concentrate on key scenes in the classroom and either summarize large portions of the play or assign take-home reading.

Excerpting a play takes some skill and thought, but there are many "key scenes" posted online that are strong excerpts that might help you to get started. When excerpting a scene, it is always best to consider whether the excerpt can make sense on its own; that is, it can stand alone as a little story unto itself. When excerpting, strive to keep the exchange short and manageable for students, but interesting enough to keep them challenged and engaged. Remember, there is no magic length. This will help your struggling readers manage understanding, and it will allow them to move onto developing critical-thinking skills. Likewise, a more focused excerpt will allow your higher-performing readers to dig more deeply into the text to unlock its more complex elements, literary devices, and subtle inferential messages without being overwhelmed by volume.

A well-selected excerpt frames a central dilemma or a bold action. If we use that excerpt as the starting point for a unit, we engage students in the most interesting and vivid moment(s) of the play. In doing so, we haven't "spoiled" the ending. When we study history, we all know how the story will turn out. Instead, the work in studying history is being able to examine what preceded the event, how the event or situation escalated, and the outcome of the event. An excerpt from a play can make a strong impact on a learner. Don't be afraid to dive into a chunk of a play that helps students develop thinking skills in relation to learning targets.

Use History Plays Like Time Machines

We read history; we watch plays. Using a scene, a monologue, or parts of a play to bring history to life engages students in actively participating in a different moment in time. When students enter into a play, it's like they are going into a time machine. They travel back to reconstructed historical scenes with their present day mindset. This time travel allows students to make immediate interdisciplinary connections between history and art, fiction and non-fiction. The idea of traveling back in time allows students to see how themes in history can be examined or evaluated from a contemporary viewpoint. Actively approaching social studies is a very different instructional choice from traditional Social Studies classrooms that ask students to sit, read quietly, and then answer a bunch of questions in a packet or in the back of a textbook. Let's not do that anymore! Students need to experience history, not just read about it.

Beginning a study of history by acting out parts of a play is one simple way to begin to build interdisciplinary connections for students, demonstrating ways in which art can help students enter into social studies. We have discussed that work in other chapters, and we hope that has helped to shape more dynamic lessons.

Get students on their feet performing parts of history found in dramatic literature. This is an excellent "springboard strategy" into a unit of study. Students can actually become the historical figure, which is very different from reading about historical figures. Beginning a unit of social studies in an active way, allows students to see history, hear history, and feel history. These are three important learning qualities that can hook a learner, encouraging students to be transported to a different moment in time.

On the Broad Level: Springboard into History at Its Most Exciting Moments

On the broad level: Where to start? Begin with choosing a scene or an excerpt from a play that is the *most* interesting portion of the play: a scene that has the most relevance to your lesson and learning targets. Remember, the excerpt can be from the beginning, middle, or end of the play. The key is to find a scene in the play that is highly engaging for students.

This suggestion is a break in traditional teaching and learning practices. Most educators start all things from the beginning. They think that a full context needs to be established in order for the most "spectacular" moments to make sense. When we consider history and social studies, we need to think differently about why and how we study events in time. The event itself is only a culmination to a much larger story. Examining the exposition and outcomes of history is what demands critical thinking and more demanding thinking. This effort allows for students to identify and examine the culminating details that lead up to a historical event. It allows students to think about how events are sequenced, make connections to details, and expose elements of history that shape a moment in time or shape the future.

On the Broad Level: Use Play Excerpts to Provide a Historical Overview

Breaking with tradition. Many of us think it is necessary for students to read every word of a story or play—from start to finish. This is not necessary when building interdisciplinary connections. Skip big chunks and get to the most engaging part(s) of the play that make logical sense for your lesson plans and learning targets.

Like using an excerpt from a play to springboard into a historical discussion, like a time traveler, consider how excerpts from plays can be used in other ways to provide a complete overview of history in a short amount of time. Like in the springboard example, you might choose to work with the full class on one area of the play, which might help to focus the students on something specific, but you might choose to work with collaborative groups, where each group explores a different scene within a play and then presents that scene to the class. For instance, if you have five groups, you could choose five different scenes and cover an entire span of history by using those scenes to overview the social studies unit.

More Specifically: Unpack Social Issues

Forward thinking Social Studies curricula foster students' abilities to see history and sociology from multiple viewpoints. Hindsight is 20/20, and plays about history reveal those viewpoints. Historical plays supply a narrative, but they often supply a counter-narrative, a viewpoint that defies long-standing, sanitized descriptions of history, culture, and events.

When we make use of plays in a social studies classroom, we are looking to: (1) question value assumptions; (2) compare texts of opposing cultural values; (3) experience stories written by ethnic writers that explore marginalized groups within a culture; (4) raise awareness of contradictions; (5) reveal universality; (6) examine aspects of life that are left out. For these reasons and for many others, making interdisciplinary connections can help us to educate stronger, more socially responsible citizens. Our examples of interdisciplinary activities work to reflect one or more of these six characteristics.

As we consider current thematic and meaningful discussions with students about social studies and an interdisciplinary approach to social studies, we'd like to focus on four important, long-standing concerns of the Social Studies classroom: segregation, prejudice, harassment, and genocide. There are many others, but we start with these four because they cover a range of units familiar to most Social Studies curricula. While we consider these four areas, we will look at important interdisciplinary connections that help students to navigate their thinking, question, and conduct meaningful and relevant research. These suggestions are meant to be starting points for developing stronger connections between fiction and non-fiction. The next step would be building them into curricular units that best suit students and a school's curriculum objectives.

Use Plays to Establish a Different Viewpoint on Segregation
Recommended plays: *A Raisin in the Sun* and *Clybourne Park*
Segregation is a difficult concept for students to understand:

- ◆ How and why does it occur?
- ◆ When are efforts to desegregate successful? Why?
- ◆ When are they not? Why?

These are higher-order, critical-thinking questions that require an interdisciplinary approach. We cannot come to examine the concept of segregation by simply looking at the demographic distribution of our population. The concerns of segregation go much deeper than seeing populations congregating on a map.

Segregation is also tied to racism, and socio-economic and sociological factors. In a traditional Social Studies classes, segregation is often studied detached from the stories of real people. The human effect of segregation is not exposed, and the effects of segregation are not confronted. Plays offer insights into the stories of segregation. These stories open up the opportunity to gain insight into the human and cultural effects of segregation. Lorainne Hansberrry's A *Raisin in the Sun* and Bruce Norris' play *Clybourne Park* are two excellent plays to connect students to stories with segregation as strong curricular tie to social studies.

Interdisciplinary Activities and Questions

1. In relation to the play, have students study specific neighborhoods in the area in which individuals live. In what ways do those neighborhoods reflect culture, race, politics, or socio-economic status. Have small groups of students develop a report about particular neighborhoods that surround them: what is the neighborhood's history, its demographics, and its descriptive characteristics. In what ways do neighbors change over time? How does the play convey the impact of segregation? This activity is particularly rich in urban settings; however, it is equally revealing to study differing neighborhoods and communities across our country.

2. In relation to the play, have students interview individuals about their perspectives on segregation. As a class, construct a survey of questions to ask varying age groups what they know about segregation and their thoughts about segregation. Some groups could survey individuals who are within the age ranges 15–20, 20–30, 40–50, 50–60, or 60 and older. Strive to gain a range of understanding of segregation and our values and belief systems. Consider the collected data with the thoughts and opinions revealed by the author of the play and his/her characters.

3. Examine current practices of segregation in schools. Examine the differences in those schools by reviewing school report card data related to demographics and performance. Have students speculate on the educational effects of segregation. How are these effects and concerns similar or different from the concerns explored in the plays?

4. Create and debate policies around segregation. What are politicians saying now and in the past? The Supreme Court? Local government? How are those ideas swayed? How does the reading of a play sway students' opinions or thoughts related to segregation?

5. Explore the universal effects of segregation. A large or small group discussion of this topic could include the following questions:

   o In what ways does segregation erode a democratic culture?
   o What are the contradictions of segregation in a democracy?
   o How does the play exhibit those contradictions?
   o How do those contradictions show up in the characters, their circumstances, and conflicts?

Use Plays to Gain a Different Viewpoint on Prejudice

Recommended plays: *"Master Harold" . . . and the boys* and *The Normal Heart*

Students are increasingly attentive and sensitive to issues of prejudice. Often, many students have been personally affected by prejudice. As educators, approaching the reality of prejudices is a sensitive topic. We need to be aware of all students in the classroom attuned to how our discussions of prejudice may relate to their personal lives and experiences. With that said, the examination of prejudice is a topic we cannot avoid, and it is a topic of discussion that is crucial if we are going to engage in changes that defy prejudice.

On an interdisciplinary level, fiction and plays offer a vivid and often profound experience with the insidious nature of prejudice and how it affects individuals. Plays put a voice to prejudice and its role in conflict. They also provide opportunities for students to better understand and grapple with the nuances of prejudice, which they might not get by reading a piece of non-fiction or a news article about prejudice. Fiction and plays get to the human side of these stories.

Interdisciplinary Activities and Questions

1. A greater understanding of prejudices can best be heard from victims of prejudice. For this reason, we encourage reading plays written from a cultural point of view. This provides a much more authentic reference point for discussion—and offers a counter-narrative to majority culture. In this interdisciplinary commitment, compare and contrast narratives. Why and how did prejudices develop? In what ways does the fictional reading counter those prejudices and speak out against those prejudices?

2. Question value assumptions of prejudice and provide a historical review of how prejudice has manifested itself in policy and decision

making on a governmental level. Compare and contrast various cultures in relation to their views and prejudices? Where, when, and how do prejudices manifest themselves differently? In the plays you read, where, when, and how do prejudices manifest themselves and nurture conflict? How do prejudices evolve? How can we eliminate prejudice?

3. Study examples in history and in plays that contradict prejudice belief or value systems. Have students analyze the ways prejudice can be countered and create listings of ways to confront prejudice.

4. Plays often reveal what history leaves out. Have students study the play after a study of the history. In this interdisciplinary way, students should be able to identify and analyze the underlying manifestations of prejudice as the play reveals those nuances within character and conflict development. The skill of inference can be thoughtfully approached here.

5. Have students create an understanding of the universality of prejudice. If there are so many prejudices . . . is prejudice a shared, universal concern or not? Debate. Explore the patterns of prejudice that appear in non-fiction and fiction. What does prejudice look like, sound like, and feel like in non-fiction and in fiction. What are steps to combat the universality of prejudice?

Use Plays to Study the Role of Harassment in Culture
Recommended plays: *The Crucible, My Kind of Town, The Laramie Project*

Harassment in our culture continues to be its own, unregulated force. Taking many different forms, we witness harassment in a variety of different ways, from bullying to violence. Some say we are often desensitized to harassment because of its pervasiveness. When we read about harassment, we often do not stop and think about its effect. When unchecked, harassment spreads and often escalates to greater violence and even death. Good plays that expose patterns of harassment provide students with insights into the role harassment can play in our culture and the havoc it can bring into communities.

Interdisciplinary Activities and Questions
1. Students should collect a range of examples of harassment from newspapers and history. Have students put those examples on a continuum, and have them explain how harassment varies in degrees. Why is one from of harassment more severe than another form of harassment? What justifies their thinking? Then, compare the moments in the play that sequence the escalation of harassment

up against that continuum. Students should debate and discuss their perceptions around harassment.

2. From a variety of different points in time, examine the varying roles of harassment: the perpetrators, the victims, the confronters, and the bystanders. Have students identify these differing roles and compare and contrast the function of these roles in different situations. Then, have them identify these differing roles in a play and how characters operate as perpetrators of prejudice, victims, confronters, and bystanders. Expose the way these characters operate and consider why they operate in the way they do. What are the nuances that demonstrate their roles and choices?

3. When reading the play, try to connect the characters to populations they represent. Often, when we read a play or watch a film, we forget that the characters are telling the stories of not just one but of many. Ask students to make a connection between the main characters and real life, everyday people they represent. Provide questions that encourage students to analyze how and why they make the connections they do.

4. Have students research the laws regarding harassment at the time and setting of the play. For instance, what laws were and were not in place to prevent or prosecute harassment at the time. With the play, apply the laws that are actual to the time and setting of the play, then apply the law of how it has changed. Likewise, with a newer play, consider how contemporary characters might be judged using older, more antiquated laws. This activity can help students to see the way that thinking evolves inside legislation.

5. Have students research when laws of harassment have changed and at what point did our culture say "enough is enough . . . this harassment is wrong." In other words, what was the tipping point that led to a public outcry or a serious judgment against harassment? How might the play highlight the value of the law or judgment?

Use Plays to Expose the Stories of Internment and Genocide

Recommended plays: *Diary of Anne Frank* and *A Shayna Maidel*

Internment and genocide frame some of the most horrific and tragic stretches of human history. Historians strive to document these events to provide us with insights into how these events escalated to the point of such human tragedy. But fiction, while exposing the tragedies of internment and genocide, often seeks to examine the capacity of the human spirit, survival, durability, crisis of faith, family, and reconnection. As we consider these topics, we need to pay close attention to the embedded complexities of internment and genocide alongside the capacity of the human spirit to prevail. *The Diary of Anne Frank* and *A Shayna Maidel* expose both the fear and destruction around human tragedy, but they also explore survival, the power of human spirit, and the hope of reconnection.

Interdisciplinary Activities and Questions

1. Conduct a research study of the survivors of internment or genocide. What are their stories of survival? Where did they find refuge and how did they live through the horror of the circumstances they were under? How did they endure, and in what ways did they continue to suffer? What were/are the lasting effects? How does the play examine the capacity of survival and what does the play reveal about the strength of human endurance?

2. Examine how and why governments condone internment or genocide. Why is it allowed to happen and not stopped? What characteristics of the time allow for these atrocities? Compare these governments with governments in opposition. What, if any, do some governments offer as reparations for a survivor? Why and how are those reparations justified? What types of policies can be created in order to monitor and put an end to genocide?

3. The Shoah Foundation and the United States Holocaust Memorial Museum offer a variety of films for classroom use documenting the testimonies of holocaust survivors that can be used in conjunction with the recommended plays. Watch excerpts of those media texts to address the following questions: What are some of the long-term effects of internment or genocide? How should the country be held accountable for acts of internment or genocide?

4. Study the role of a "crisis of faith" and explain how the human spirit can be broken under certain regimes. What does it mean to have a crisis of faith, and how does the author of the play delve into the crisis to expose elements of despair that a history textbook cannot expose? Consider doing a comparison of a non-fiction reading to an excerpted play. What does one excerpt reveal? What does the fiction passage excerpt reveal?

5. Research real life stories of families and reconnections after a genocide or holocaust. What circumstances brought families back together? What are some of ironies of those stories? Have students write a dialogue or script about these families reconnecting. What would they say to one another after all of those years?

Building interdisciplinary experiences for students might seem like a difficult and added challenge for the work of teaching, but it doesn't need to be. Start simply. Make the effort to help students draw associations that engage the learner and force them to make critical-thinking connections that represent the higher-order, critical-thinking skills we are trying to build into our classrooms. As the interdisciplinary connections become more apparent, more interesting questions and project-based learning activities can be developed, often to connect with real life, current events. Remember, the work of "making connections" should be left to the student—teaching doesn't mean telling and identifying connections for students. Challenge students to research and to make the connections that stand out to them. Allowing students to explore these interdisciplinary associations on their own or in their collaborative groups fosters enriching ideas, judgments, and evaluative skills that students need to demonstrate as we push our students' greater potential.

Opportunity for Reflection

Consider how you might apply ideas from this chapter to your own classroom.

1. What is the purpose of interdisciplinary activities or projects? Why is it important for students to see a relationship between fiction and non-fiction?
2. How does your unit reflect: (a) how we question value assumptions; (b) comparing texts of opposing cultural values; (c) hearing stories written by ethnic writers not just about ethnic issues; (d) raising awareness of contradictions; (e) revealing universality; (f) examining aspects of life that are left out.
3. In what ways can students learn to be more reflective and empathetic during an interdisciplinary learning experience? In what ways can you recognize that level of learning and provide the student with feedback that reinforces higher-order, critical-thinking skills?
4. When working with complex social concerns, ask students to think on better resolutions to current concerns they face or they hear about in the news? How does the studying of the play inform their own approach to these complex social concerns?

8

Measuring Growth: Activities for Exploration, Reflection, and Assessment

Reading dramatic literature has long been a staple of the ELA curricula. Bringing play scripts into a social studies classroom or performing scenes from those dramatic texts in either ELA or social studies classrooms may not be business as usual in most curricula, but writing, speaking, and critical-thinking activities certainly are stressed in both academic areas. Writing and speaking activities facilitate a more seamless integration of active approaches to dramatic literature into the objectives and outcomes of established curricula. The activities presented in this chapter can be sequenced into preview, formative, and summative experiences. The selection of specific activities for previewing, exploration, reflection, and assessment is dictated by the nature of the play, the existing curriculum's objectives, and the expectations for long-range student outcomes linked to specific local and national learning standards.

Setting the Stage for Exploration: Previewing the Play, Its Issues, and Themes

Activity #1: Previewing a Text Using Opinionaires

To foster students' investment in any course of study, they should see a strong connection to their own interests and life experiences. Once properly engaged, students can dive into the subject matter using a variety of strategies to go beyond just recognizing that personal connection to a play, its themes, social issues, or historical period.

An "opinionaire" helps students articulate their views related to key interpersonal conflicts, social issues, and literary themes explored by a dramatic text. To introduce a play like *A Raisin in the Sun* students need to examine their attitudes towards the possibilities and limits of realizing the American Dream as dictated by the social norms of a specific era such as the 1950s. Beginning the opinionaire with several open-ended questions encourages students to make a connection between the past and present based on their own impressions related to what they have heard, read, or viewed at home, in school, and through the media before tackling the individual items:

◆ What do you believe characterized life in the 1950s for a working class family in Chicago?
◆ In the 1950s, how would the family's race have limited or expanded their economic opportunities?
◆ What do you believe would make life different in the 1950s in comparison to life in 2013?

The opinionaire used during TimeLine Theatre's Living History residency for this play polled the following points.

A Raisin in the Sun Opinionaire

Respond to these statements using the following scale:

5 = Strongly Agree 4 = Agree 3 = Neither agree nor disagree 2 = Disagree 1 = Strongly Disagree

◆ In the 1950s, all racial, ethnic, and economic groups enjoyed some level of the economic prosperity offered in post-war America.
◆ In the 1950s, for most families realizing the American Dream involved owning a house rather than renting an apartment.
◆ In the 1950s, households that included an extended family provided greater emotional support for its members and helped them take more risks to get ahead socially and economically.
◆ In the 1950s, the belief in God bound families (and communities) together and sustained them in times of doubt and struggle.
◆ In the 1950s, owning a small business was a better path to financial security and success rather than working for someone else.

◆ In the 1950s, earning a college diploma was the most important means to achieve career success and financial security.

◆ In the 1950s, women who pursued an education in order to commit to a career rather than to marriage risked alienating themselves from their family and their community.

◆ In the 1950s, even in times of economic struggle a man's children were a source of pride and comfort that he could leave as a meaningful legacy other than financial gain or success.

◆ In the 1950s, family decisions made by the head of the family were respected and were rarely challenged due to the respect family elders enjoyed.

◆ In the 1950s, prosperous, close-knit neighborhoods attracted families and businesses that were very similar in race, religion, or ethnicity.

◆ In the 1950s, the financial success of working class families that lifted them out of financial struggle was admired and celebrated by others who still experienced that struggle.

◆ In the 1950s, recognizing strong connections between themselves and their African heritage emerged as a source of pride and strength for Blacks.

This opinionaire uses "In the 1950s" as part of each stem in order to remind students that they are making judgments based on race relations and socio-economic conditions of a time past, not the present.

Once students have expressed their opinions using the 5–1 scale surveying the scope of historical circumstances, social issues, and literary themes presented in the play, the tool should provide a simple means for students to analyze or summarize their responses. The summary questions for the *Raisin* opinionaire include:

◆ Of the statements made about the 1950s, which one do you think is *still remains true* about those circumstances today?

◆ Why do you think those circumstances have not changed in more than 50 years?

Debriefing the Opinionaire

Option #1: A Raise of Hands

Discussions based on the opinionaire's results could begin simply with students raising their hands in response to how they applied the scale to key items, which allows the teacher and the entire class to gain a snapshot impression of student responses.

Option #2: A Human Barometer

We also have used a "human barometer" approach to polling the class, which gets students on their feet after a few ensemble building warm-ups. Create a barometer, or continuum, where "strongly agree" is established on one side of the classroom and "strongly disagree" is established on the other side. Have students move to a position on that invisible continuum as you read the items listed on the opinionaire. We have also experimented with having each item come up as a projected slide to complement reading them aloud.

Initial polling of the entire class, using either option, allows everyone to express their opinions without necessarily being singled out in discussion. Then, the class can move on to discussing the item that had the most and least amount of consensus.

Variation: Creating a Gallery of Opinions

When introducing *The Normal Heart* to high school classrooms, teachers may be concerned about students' ability and willingness to discuss a play that featured not only gay men, but gay men who were under siege by the ravages of AIDS as well as the loss of friends and loved ones to that disease. In addition to creating an opinionaire to tackle attitudes towards gay lifestyles and AIDS advocacy, the teachers can focus on one of the play's themes, the desire to maintain control in a crisis and the loss of it on a variety of levels.

When constructing strategies for this discussion, the primary aim should become helping students make personal connections to the play that don't rely solely on their attitudes towards sexual orientation. Also, the strategy for sharing the results of this modified opinionaire activity first encourages quiet reflection and then individually processing other students' responses. This approach attempts to foster tolerance of others' opinions and resisting swift, as well as not fully informed or considered, responses.

This activity asks students to briefly write about particular times in their life when they have felt powerless, a state that many of the characters in the play encounter at one time or another. Students write for three to five minutes on the following topics:

- ◆ I felt that I had the least amount of power or control at home when . . .
- ◆ I felt that I had the least amount of power or control at school when . . .
- ◆ I felt that I had the least amount of power or control in a friendship when . . .
- ◆ I felt I had the least amount of power or control over my body or my health when . . .

Depending on how students feel about engaging in a high level of self-disclosure, their responses could be shared anonymously in several ways. One strategy, using index cards, permits students to write their responses giving them just a small, less intimidating space to fill. The cards could be posted as a gallery of responses on a classroom bulletin board or wall. Students then select the cards that they feel the most comfortable sharing and post them on the bulletin board or wall. The class would read the responses of fellow students in a silent "gallery walk."

Once the gallery walk has concluded, students will select one card (not their own) that they find the most interesting or relevant to their own experience and write a reaction on the back of the card. The teacher may need to set parameters about what that reaction should include: for example, a connection to their own experience, some constructive advice, or personal affirmation. Once a reaction has been crafted, the card would go back on the wall for "pick up" by the original responder or each "reacting" student would read the card that they picked off the gallery wall and their response.

Opinionaires can be used once again at the end of the unit to measure how much students' attitudes have changed once they have read the play, studied a character, and performed a scene as well as seen the play in performance at the theater or in a film version. Students can reflect on the difference between the "pre" and "post" response to the opinionaire in either a class discussion or a written reflection piece.

Activity #2: Previewing the Play's Language, Characters, and Themes

Before students read the play, teachers can select a range of quotations from the text that represent the major characters and the language that turn themes into dialogue and action. The individual quotations are scattered on the floor or on a table. Small groups sift through the quotations and create thematic "categories" that link related quotations together. For example, in the dramatization of Chaim Potok's novel *My Name Is Asher Lev*, students would find individual quotations that focus on religious identity, the meaning of artistic expression, and the struggle to maintain one's identity amid the expectations of family and community. It would be the students' task to group individual quotations as they discover those thematic patterns. Teachers can certainly make suggestions of possible themes, perhaps the first time this strategy is used, but there really isn't any pressure to identify the "correct" themes initially. As students read the play and see these lines of dialogue in context, they can return to this opening activity and examine which themes resonated when those ideas were encountered out of their proper context and refine their articulation of the theme developed by a set of isolated lines.

Activity #3: Previewing the Play's Theme Through Poetry Analysis

Many playwrights, as well as novelists, use a poem as the inspiration for a title in order to establish an intertextual link between the two works or to reveal a thematic connection to that poem. Consider again *A Raisin in the Sun*. Lorraine Hansberry's title makes an allusion to a line in Langston Hughes' poem, "Harlem," which begins with the rhetorical question, "What happens to a dream deferred?" It then expands and explores that central question with five subsequent questions including, "Does it dry up/like a raisin in the sun?" Those questions rephrase and respond to the initial one using a series of powerful metaphors and a tragic consequence, *"Does it explode?"* This poem offers several opportunities to engage students in one of the central issues of the play: what happens when individual characters come up against obstacles that prevent them from realizing their dreams in part or in full?

TimeLine Theatre's lobby display for this play featured an enlarged copy of Hughes' poem that was flanked by audience responses to two questions: What dream of yours has come true? What dream has been deferred? Creating such a display in the classroom could reflect students' responses to those questions. They later can examine the aspirations and obstacles of characters in the play and use the display to "pin" characters' responses to those questions over the course of reading the play and rehearsing their scenes.

Another of Hughes' poems, "Mother to Son," provides an opportunity to introduce a poem that takes the form of a dramatic monologue and presents an extended metaphor, a staircase embodying a mother's journey through life: "Life for me ain't been no crystal stair." Examining that poem allows students to not only discuss the worldview expressed by the poem's speaker but provides an opportunity to model the poem. They can create an original extended metaphor to represent what their life's journey has been or what they hope it can be in the future.

Once students begin reading the play and examining its characters, they should come back to both poems and discuss how specific characters would react to the poems' subjects and themes. Students again could model the poems, this time using one of the play's characters to inform the content of that revised version.

Activity #4: Previewing the Play's Historical Period Through Images

In order to prepare to study Aaron Posner's adaptation of *My Name of Asher Lev*, presenting a series of images of the neighborhood that Asher inhabited in post-World War II Brooklyn helps students visualize his world. Those images can showcase not only the neighborhood environment but the clothing, the social interactions, and the religious rituals of a community and lifestyle that might be difficult for students to visualize readily based on their own personal experiences and media representation of that cultural group. Students can gather their own images for a particular play including photographs, paintings, sketches, sculpture, among other types of visual material by conducting an online search. This online research activity provides students an opportunity to review effective ways to access visual information online, select reliable sources, and choose an appropriate range of examples that could be assembled as a slide show or set of printed images for display as a classroom gallery.

Activity #5: Using Film Trailers and Television Programs as a Previewing Tool

Since many plays take readers back to past historical periods and events, teachers can make effective use of any number of programs from PBS, The History Channel, or HBO's extensive short documentary collection. When preparing to study the play, *The Triangle Factory Fire Project*, students can experience a visual history lesson by viewing *Triangle Fire* from the PBS *American Experience* series. The program's webpage offers a wide range of bonus videos, including a preview of the episode, interactive tools, and print articles. Many PBS programs are available for free of charge streaming at their parent series' website. Usually programs like *Triangle Fire* lend themselves to easy excerpting, and those segments can be integrated gradually into a residency or curriculum unit as particular aspects of an historical event or social issue become relevant.

During a unit focusing on *The Triangle Factory Fire Project*, a trailer for *The True Cost*, a film about today's "fast fashion" industry and its reliance on cheap, exploited labor connects an incident from the past with similar problems in the present day as part of several anticipatory activities prior to reading the script. Well-designed documentary trailers are created to capture the viewer's attention, introduce the film's thesis, and provide key images and sound bites to preview how that thesis will be explored. Using a trailer to introduce an historical or social issue makes for an effective discussion starter. Students can carefully analyze the content of the trailer to determine what still needs to be learned or discovered that cannot be covered in a highly condensed preview such as a trailer. Filling in the gaps of needed information could come once the television program or film is screened in its entirety in one or several class periods, or it can be the springboard for online research and close reading of selected, related non-fiction and primary sources. Using a trailer as a means to gain an overview of a film parallels how reading or viewing a play that tackles a social issue or controversial event can stimulate audience questions and curiosity to learn more about that issue or event.

Character Development Activities for Deeper Exploration and as Formative Assessment Tools

When students are assigned a character to track through reading the text and/or rehearsing a specific scene from a play, the following formative activities can be effective means to assess how well a student understands a particular character. These formative assessment tools require close reading of the play to extract textual support as well as a good deal of inferencing based on the discovered clues from dialogue and stage directions. While not only serving as formative assessment tools during the reading and rehearsal of a play, they also function as pre-writing experiences for more sophisticated capstone writing experiences after reading, performing, and possibly viewing the play on film or in a theater.

Activity #6: Creating a Character Dossier

Students can investigate their assigned characters by examining a specific scene or the play as a whole for clues to create the character's history or backstory. This is part of an actor's preparation for a role prior to and throughout the rehearsal process. The Character Dossier activity requires close reading of the text to pick up information that fills in the blanks of the dossier's item stems (see Handout 8.1) as well as necessitates students making inferences based on textual support for details that are not explicitly stated in the dialogue.

Extension: Creating a Time Capsule or Treasure Box

As an extension of the Character Dossier activity, students can prepare a time capsule or treasure box that contains five artifacts including one piece of writing that would either be prepared by the character or something written by someone else that has meaning for the character. Students should consider how the time capsule or treasure box represents not only the character but the play's time period as well. The time capsule could be represented by the actual items or by pictures of them. No matter what form the capsule or box takes, it should be supplemented with a written explanation of why those items were selected, preferably written from the character's perspective. This activity could be linked to the "That's My Bag" speech discussed later in this chapter.

Extension: Creating a Coat of Arms

Students also could create a "coat of arms" based on the decisions they make for their character completing the dossier. Coat of Arms templates are easily found online at the ReadWriteThink website. One reproducable template is included as a handout at the end of the chapter (Handout 8.2). Most templates divide the shield into four or six sections. It would be up to the teacher or students to determine what information is included in each of the sections, and those categories could come from the stems used in the character dossier. A variation on how to represent a character using the coat of arms template might rely solely on images or a combination of images and text.

A display of completed coats of arms makes an effective gallery walk experience. The display might group different versions for a single character together and clearly identify who is being represented, or they could be displayed in a random manner without identifying the character so students would have to decide which characters belonged to specific coats of arms.

Activity #7: Creating a Character Portrait—A Picture Is Worth a Thousand Words

Building on the use of images to help with actors' preparation, students can design and execute three to five photos that would act as an articulation of "visual resume" to represent their character's social status, family situation, ambitions, and personal struggles. A line of dialogue, either spoken by or about the character, would accompany each image. A natural extension for writing would encourage students to explain their planning (setting/environment, costume, props, pose) for each image and submit a portfolio of their images and with their explanation. This activity also allows for a gallery walk display or a slide show for easy sharing.

Activity #8: Public Speaking and Role-Playing

A speech called "That's My Bag" has been used as an icebreaker activity at the beginning of a school term, as well as to prepare students for memoir writing by teachers at Adlai E. Stevenson High School. This activity builds on the decisions made in the Character Dossier activity and it transfers well to improvisational role-playing activities where students demonstrate the depth of their understanding of a character. That improvisational activity could take the form of a talk show, a town hall meeting, or a trial.

Step #1: Brainstorming

Students begin the process with a brainstorming step, which requires them to list ten things that have special meaning to their character. Those things could be objects, clothing, books, letters, jewelry, etc. Students write briefly about at least five of the things on their list to explain why each item has special meaning for their character. Since students speak as the character, they should write about the significance of the things from the character's point of view. Then, students would share at least one item on their list with the class as a whole, to a partner or in a small group.

Step #2: Narrowing the Focus, Developing the Speech's Content

In order to determine the content of the three- to five-minute speech, students select three things (that they could easily bring to class) that define various aspects of the character's lives, personality, relationships, etc. They build an anecdote around each thing based on textual evidence or inference and link the anecdotes together. To further develop the speech, it needs an attention getter and a controlling idea/thesis to create the introduction, a developed body that gives balanced attention to each thing selected, appropriate transitions between anecdotes, and a conclusion, which ideally links back to the attention getter. Students will probably need to be coached to keep in mind that the speech needs a clear strategy or premise to link all three things. For example, a student could choose three "hats" to indicate the various roles their characters play during the course of the play and explain where and why that character wears each hat.

Step #3: Establishing Norms for Delivering the Speech

Setting standards for the speech's delivery should be at the discretion of the classroom teacher based on how much formal and informal public speaking students have experienced in other curricular units. Adaptable public speaking rubrics are available at https://www.edutopia.org/ and can be easily adapted to the assignment and to students' abilities. When evaluating the content of the speech, teachers should focus on how well students' choices are informed by textual evidence and careful inferencing based on that evidence.

Not one of these formative activities involves a traditional multiple choice or essay test, but students' understanding of the play's content and the development of a specific character can be assessed effectively based on the resulting products using a variety of modes (writing, speaking, media production). The classroom teacher can use those results to modify instruction as needed, as with any formative assessment tool. Activities presented here can be modified to include content that is specific to the host class whether it is a literature, sociology, government, or psychology class in order to assess whether effective connections are being made between the content of the play and course-specific concepts.

Capstone Writing Activities

The capstone activities draw on a variety of formative assessment experiences such as developing a Character Dossier or conducting research about an issue, time period, or event central to a given play. Students would demonstrate an ability to analyze and/or synthesize information into a more developed and sustained response to the play or their experience inhabiting a specific character through the classroom rehearsal process. These writing activities provide a means of summative assessment since they require students to demonstrate a high level of recall and understanding of the play's content as well as the play's historical context, literary themes, and social issues.

Essay Topic #1: Analyzing a Character

The Character Dossier activity easily adapts to a more formal character analysis essay. Depending upon the type of classroom and curriculum, this analysis might trace the character's growth over the course of encountering the play's conflict. The analysis would assess the degree to which the character emerges as dynamic or static by facing the play's conflict and how their position in the play as protagonist, antagonist, or character foil helps to develop other major and minor characters. It could take on a speculative approach by not only examining what the character says and does onstage but how that information helps the reader, viewer, and actor imagine how the character's onstage behavior will propel them into an imagined future. This speculative approach would be grounded in specific textual evidence. When assessing this formalized character analysis built upon the Character Dossier, the teacher would consider how well the writer integrates details developed in that formative activity and from specific textual support.

Essay Topic #2: Examining Levels of Conflict

If a play is studied as part of a sociology or psychology class, a capstone writing experience for those students might carefully examine the levels of conflict present in a play through lenses specific to those academic disciplines. Rebecca Gilman's *Spinning into Butter* provides an ideal catalyst for this approach. The play focuses on a counselor at a liberal arts college in New England who must cope with racist attacks on a black student as she faces her deeply entrenched yet artfully sublimated personal prejudices. Her public and private behavior puts her at odds with both the students and her colleagues. That scenario provides the context to examine the levels of conflict embedded in the play based on the following scheme:

Interpersonal	Conflicts that arise from relationships in families, and between friends or co-workers.
Intrapersonal	Conflicts that are more internalized but revealed/articulated through subtext or from explicit self-disclosure.
Societal	Conflicts that are imposed on individuals by the values and expectations of their social/cultural groups.

Examining a play using this approach requires students to carefully consider the complexity of characterization and plotting of events, which reveals and develops these levels to elucidate the play's essential themes. Students can bring concepts gleaned from the study of psychology or sociology to bear on their analysis as well as integrate information contained in non-fiction print and non-print texts found in the dramaturgical packet. *Inana* by Michele Lowe also suits this essay topic particularly well. The play centers on an imperiled ancient statue of the goddess Inana that sheds light on the personal and cultural struggles of Middle Eastern women. This cultural conflict is set within the story of a newly wedded couple coming to understand the implications of their arranged marriage in saving both that statue and the wife who is imperiled in her home country for teaching women to read. This topic could be applied to canonical ELA plays like *The Crucible* or *A Raisin in the Sun* and could replace more traditional approaches to the character analysis essay.

Essay Topic #3: Responding to a Social Issue

Many of the plays focus on a social issue such as calling the public, government, and medical community to respond to the HIV/AIDS crisis in the early 1980s. *The Normal Heart* stimulates a discussion of how that crisis has evolved over time leading to better understanding of not only the disease but the personal toll it takes on its victims and their loved ones. Having students identify and research "case studies" that relate to the central social issue or problem that forms the central conflict of a play would yield a means to continue the conversation that the play starts. For *The Normal Heart*, Ryan White's story created the opportunity to explore how his experiences were represented through a full spectrum of media coverage and that coverage's impact on the public's response to the AIDS crisis as it persisted through 1980s. As students conduct an online search for print and non-print sources that cover Ryan's story, involving someone close to their age, they would be guided by a set of preliminary questions:

◆ Why did it take Ryan White to raise consciousness about HIV/AIDS?
◆ How did Ryan White put a "face" on the HIV/AIDS crisis in the 1980s?
◆ Why was it easier to discuss the nature of the disease, its transmission, its treatment, and its social consequences through the lens of Ryan White's struggle to attend public school than the effect of the disease on the gay community?
◆ To what extent was Ryan's case the best lens for America to engage in conversation about this public health issue?

In addition to the questions posed here, students would be encouraged to add to questions that emerge from their research. Those questions will guide how they transform their research into an essay that examines the role Ryan White's story played in advancing awareness of the disease's reach and creating a call to action in developing treatment of AIDS. Students could research the same case study as a class or they could research other celebrities, sports figures, and activists like Arthur Ashe, Magic Johnson, Rock Hudson, and Elizabeth Glazer individually or in small groups.

Journalistic Writing: Understanding the Historical Period

A capstone writing activity doesn't necessarily take the form of an essay, either narrative or argumentative. In a social studies class, there might be a different emphasis on students demonstrating their understanding of an historical period or a dramatic text that goes beyond the limits of the essay form. Since a class's online research can provide students with a wealth of historical information, students could transform that information into a variety of journalistic writing pieces. Of course, students could create a newspaper that focuses on the central event or issue covered in the play like *The Triangle Factory Fire Project*, but this approach can be directed at analyzing particular modes of journalistic writing and style.

If a dramaturgical packet includes primary source newspaper reporting, those news stories, human-interest pieces, and editorials could be read and examined to help students test each journalistic form for the presence of bias. The lesson begins by defining the following terms: inverted pyramid reporting, bias, editorializing, straight news, hard news vs. soft news. Definitions of those terms can be accessed at The News Manual, which is billed as "A Professional Resource for Journalists and The Media."

Instead of writing newspaper stories or editorials, students could create a series of headlines that cover the events depicted in the play. Initially, students could write headlines in highly neutral language that focus on as much of the "who," "what," "where," and "when" as needed to express the event. Once those headlines are created and reviewed for their use of neutral language, students would switch headlines and add loaded language to sensationalize the headline. When the headlines are revised, they should be pooled together and then ranked from most to least sensational. Students should select headlines that capture the tone of the play as a whole or that reflect particular characters' responses at key points in the play. And, using historical facts surrounding the events of the play, a variety of newspaper articles could be written based on those headlines to capture the level of bias they express.

This activity works well to assess how well students understand which events shape the plot and conflict of the play as well as their ability to manipulate word choice in order to achieve a specific effect first to maintain neutrality and then to express a certain degree of bias or outright sensationalism of the tabloid press.

Bringing It All Together

These activities aim to extend the analysis of any play, blending the work of a student actor who is delving deeper into a character and exploring the historical and/or political context of the play with formative and summative assessment tools involving speaking and writing rather than testing. The suggestions presented here can easily be mixed and matched to suit the abilities and interests of students and your aims as a teacher willing to blend innovative and traditional techniques to bring literary themes, social issues, and history alive.

Opportunity for Reflection

Consider how you might apply ideas from this chapter to your own classroom.

1. How do you typically assess students' prior knowledge before beginning a unit of study?
2. And once that assessment is applied, how do you build on that prior knowledge?
3. How do you adjust your strategies based on that assessment of students' prior knowledge?
4. What activities do you implement that require students to use critical and imaginative thinking to dig more deeply into the circumstances and implications of a text?
5. To what extent is there a clear connection between activities presented throughout a unit to provide students the opportunity for preview, exploration, and reflection?
6. How can writing activities, in place of a multiple choice test, yield a comparable means to measure students' knowledge and understanding at the culmination of a unit?

Handout 8.1: Character Dossier

My name is:

My parents are:

I have_____brother(s) and _____ sister(s).

I was born in _____ on_____ (date or time of year).

My first memory is:

My prized possession is:

My best friend is_____, because

I am happiest when:

I am most afraid when:

I am easily hurt when:

The secret that I have not shared with anyone is:

If I could go back in time, I would change:

When I close my eyes at night, I dream about:

The thing I most like to do is:

The thing I would most like to do for my family is:

The thing that makes me angry is:

I hope that in the future I could:

I am afraid that in the future I will not be able to:

The three words I would use to describe myself are:

Three words that my family would use to describe me are:

Handout 8.2: Coat of Arms Template

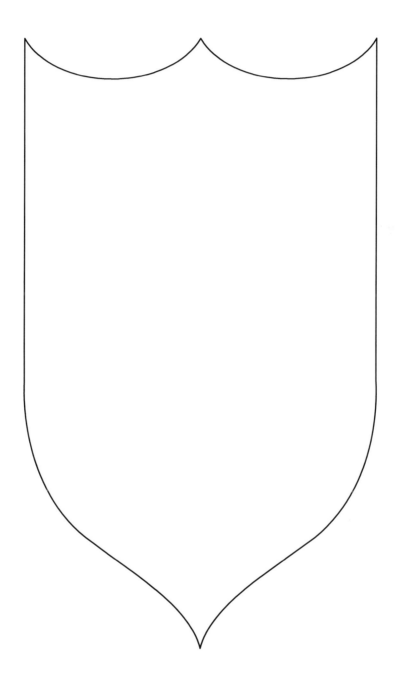

Appendix A: Lesson Plans

Lesson Plan: Reading the Entire Play

Instead of presenting a day-to-day lesson plan, this approach encourages blending active approaches with assigning students to read and discuss a play as you normally would. The first time you integrate ensemble-building activities and scenework, you may not want to tackle the dramaturgical research piece. There really is no magic solution to supplementing the core focus of "acting it out" with other viewing, research, and writing activities. Tailor those choices to the curriculum's aims and to students' abilities, needs, and interests.

Phase #1: Anticipatory activities before reading the play: 2–4 days
- Begin with "actor basics" (outlined in Chapter 3) and ensemble-building warm-ups (activities #1–#5, Chapter 3).
- Complete personal goal setting (handout, Chapter 5).
- Administer and discuss opinionaire (activity #1, Chapter 8).
- Work through representative monologue (activity #6, Chapter 3) or related poetry as a group (activity #3, Chapter 8) that previews play's major themes.
- Screen a relevant short film, film excerpt, or trailer related to play's historical period, social issue, or its playwright (activity #5, Chapter 8).
- Set an agenda and assign tasks for dramaturgical research in pairs or small groups (Chapter 6).

Conduct formative assessment activity (refer to Chapter 8 for suggestions).

Phase #2: Character work while reading and discussing the play: 2–3 days
- Continue dramaturgical research in pairs or groups and create a shareable presentation of that information: online webpage, classroom lobby display, oral presentations (Chapter 6).
- Assign characters to track throughout the play to complete character dossier (activity #6, Chapter 8).

◆ Assign scenes; begin adding character-building warm-ups (activities #1–#3, Chapter 5).
◆ Conduct a table reading (Chapter 5).

Conduct second formative assessment activity (rehearsal checklist handout, Chapter 5).

Phase #3: Scenework after reading and discussing the play: 3–4 days
◆ Rehearse and show scenes.
◆ Connect character dossier to producing visual representation (photos, treasure box) journaling as character, or character analysis essay (essay topic #1, Chapter 8).
◆ Complete self-evaluation.

Conduct summative assessment activity (refer to Chapters 5 and 8 for suggestions).

Lesson Plan: Using Selected Scenes

If exploring a play as a companion text as part of an ELA or social studies unit suits your purpose, consider how you can phase in active approaches and dramaturgical research over the course of that unit. The activities don't need to be lumped together. Phasing in attention to ensemble-building, research, and scenework makes it far more organic and less threatening to students who might initially resist taking on the role of a classroom actor.

Phase #1: Preparing for scenework: 2–3 days
◆ Frame study of key scenes within the context of an existing unit.
◆ Begin with "actor basics" (Chapter 3) and ensemble-building warm-ups (activities #1–#5, Chapter 3).
◆ Complete personal goal setting (handout, Chapter 5).
◆ Preview play's language and themes (activity #2, Chapter 8) or preview play's historical period (activity #4, Chapter 8).
◆ Provide students with a summary of the play's plot along with an abbreviated dramaturgical packet.
◆ Administer and discuss opinionaire (activity #1, Chapter 8).
◆ Work through representative monologue (activity #5, Chapter 3) or related poetry as a group that previews the play's major themes (activity #3, Chapter 8).
◆ Set an agenda and assign tasks for creating a classroom lobby display based on provided dramaturgical packet as well as additional student research (Chapter 6).

Conduct formative assessment activity (refer to Chapter 8 for suggestions).

Phase #2: Scenework: 3–4 days
◆ Continue dramaturgical research in pairs or groups and create classroom lobby display of that information (Chapter 6).
◆ Assign scenes and begin adding character-building warm-ups (activities #1–#3, Chapter 5).
◆ Conduct a table reading (Chapter 5).
◆ Rehearse scenes using the reader–feeder technique (Chapter 5).

Conduct second formative assessment activity (rehearsal checklist handout Chapter 5).

Phase #3: Sharing scenes and making connections: 2–4 days
- ◆ Show scenes to class.
- ◆ Complete self-evaluation (handout, Chapter 5).
- ◆ Make connections to other texts in an ELA unit or social issues, historical events, key concepts from social studies or interdisciplinary curriculum.
- ◆ Screen film adaptation of play based on availability.

Conduct summative assessment activity (refer to Chapters 5 and 8 for suggestions).

Appendix B: Recommended Plays

Recommended Plays: Finding the Right Fit for Any Unit

In this appendix, you will find six lists of plays that we recommend you consider for your ELA or Social Studies curriculum. The plays are organized in specific categories, but those classifications are not absolute. So if you are a Social Studies teacher, you don't need to limit your selections to the plays that we have tagged as recommended for interdisciplinary application. Skim all the lists for plays that intersect literary texts, themes, historical periods, or social issues covered in existing units.

We have included the publishers of each play. Some of the plays were about to be published when we compiled the lists, so we have listed a website that announces publication of contemporary plays. You will notice that many of the titles are available only in "acting editions" from Samuel French, Dramatists Play Service, or Dramatic Publishing, which tend to be lower in cost than many mass market paperback editions. Some plays are available in downloadable pdf editions, but we have not included that information since availability isn't always guaranteed. If you are using tablets in your classroom, some titles are available in e-book editions. Do a little publication research when you select a title to make sure which print, pdf, and digital editions are currently available.

Plays adapted into theatrical release films and television movies are tagged with information indicating the release date and the director. We highly recommend screening a television movie that documents a stage production of the play to replace students seeing a live performance of that play if that opportunity is not available. Screening a theatrical release film, certainly is a viable option, but those adaptations many times "open up" a narrative to expand the locations of action as well as alter other aspects of the narrative, since the tools of filmmaking allow for different ways to represent that passage of time and movement from place to place.

Finally, many of the plays contained in the following lists represent plays used in TimeLine Theatre's Living History residences and our own classrooms. You might notice some of the plays have also been nominated or won the Pulitzer Prize for Drama. Keep an eye out for titles that make the "short list" for the Prize as well as what is playing in local professional, community, and college theaters for inspiration as well as a chance to explore a play in class using active approaches and then to organize a trip for students to see it in production.

Canonical Works and Playwrights

A Raisin in the Sun   Lorraine Hansberry

Members of the Younger family aspire to fulfill their versions of the American Dream through either earning a college degree, becoming their own boss, or becoming homeowners, while struggling with social, racial, and familial expectations of the 1950s.

Publisher: Vintage Books
Film adaptations: 1961, directed by Daniel Petrie; 2008, directed by Kenny Leon for TV

The Miracle Worker   William Gibson

Annie Sullivan's challenges to bring communication skills to Helen Keller are dramatized along with the Keller family's struggles to accept Sullivan's unorthodox and untested methods.

Publisher: Simon and Schuster
Film adaptation: 1962, directed by Arthur Penn

The Piano Lesson   August Wilson

Set in 1936, a Pittsburgh family struggles with the legacy of their ancestor's past held in slavery and the living generation's ability to gain economic prosperity. In order to purchase the land their family once worked back in Mississippi, a prized family heirloom must be sold to raise the last bit of capital.

Publisher: Plume
Film adaptation: 1995, directed by Lloyd Richards

Twelve Angry Men   Reginald Rose

A panel of jurors must decide if a youth is guilty of stabbing a shopkeeper. Their deliberations reveal the conflicts that arise when a cross section of values, attitudes, and beliefs both support and challenge one other.

Publisher: Dramatic Publishing
Film adaptation: 1957, directed by Sidney Lumet

The Glass Menagerie   Tennessee Williams

A young man reflects on the effects of his controlling mother and his emotionally fragile sister on his aspirations to move beyond that insulating and suffocating world of unrealized dreams.

Publisher: New Directions
Film adaptations: 1950, directed by Irvin Rapper; 1973, directed by Anthony Harvey; 1987, directed by Paul Newman

All My Sons   Arthur Miller

A successful suburban businessman and his family confront the painful aftermath of World War II, yearning for the return of one son deemed missing in action and a criminal negligence suit brought against the patriarch's military supply plant. An impending marriage brings conflict not comfort to the family since it is between the surviving son and the missing brother's fiancée as well as the daughter of the plant employee who went to prison instead of the family patriarch.

Publisher: Dramatists Play Service
Film adaptation: 1948, directed by Irving Reis

Antigone   Jean Anouilh

Based on Sophocles' tragedy, Antigone challenges a fascist regime that does not allow her the personal autonomy and integrity to fulfill the demands honoring her politically rebellious brother's death that defies the prevailing civil authority that he openly challenged in battle.

Publisher: Samuel French
Film adaptation: 1974, directed by Gerald Freedman for *Great Performances* (PBS)

The Front Page   Ben Hecht and Charles MacArthur

Former reporters turned playwrights created this comedy set in the 1920s about a tabloid newspaper in Chicago. Hildy Johnson, about to move on to married life and a new career, is dragged into covering one last sensational story, when an escaped prisoner, scheduled to hang, crawls through the window of the newspaper's office.

Publisher: Samuel French
Film adaptations: 1931, directed by Lewis Milestone; 1970, directed by Alan Handley; 1974, directed by Billy Wilder; 1940, *His Girl Friday*, directed by Howard Hawks

The Little Foxes   Lillian Hellman

This family melodrama focuses on Regina Hubbard Giddens, who negotiates a bid for financial and personal independence by manipulating her husband, brothers, and their children as they all scheme to profit from the cotton industry in the New South of the early twentieth century.

Publisher: Dramatists Play Service
Film adaptation: 1941, directed by William Wyler

"Master Harold" . . . and the boys   Athol Fugard

A South African teenage finds himself under the influence of an intolerant, absent father and the compassionate, wise father figure, who happens to be a black employee in his parents' tea room. One rainy afternoon "Master Harold" tests his allegiance to those two men with startling results.

Publisher: Vintage International
Film adaptations: 1985, directed by Michael Lindsay-Hogg; 2010, directed by Lonny Price

Non-canonical Works and Playwrights

Dancing at Lughnasa   Brian Friel

Told retrospectively the adult narrator recounts the summer of 1936 in County Donegal, Ireland when he stayed with his five aunts, Mundy sisters, who are at a crossroads, personally and economically, when the local mines close, relatives return, and a marriage proposal beckons.

Publisher: Dramatists Play Service
Film adaptation: 1998, directed by Pat O'Connor

The Normal Heart   Larry Kramer

This groundbreaking drama presents members of the gay community confronting the AIDS epidemic in the early 1980s, meeting both resistance and support from the medical, legal, and civic arena to alert the public and to treat the victims.

Publisher: Samuel French
Film adaptations: 2014, directed by Ryan Murphy

The Last Night of Ballyhoo   Alfred Uhry

Set in Atlanta in December 1939, the Freitags, a highly assimilated Jewish family, are preoccupied with two significant events: the world premiere of *Gone With the Wind* and Ballyhoo, a cotillion ball at an exclusive country club. Newspapers report that Hitler has just invaded Poland. In this dramedy, the introduction of an eligible bachelor from the father's business provides a catalyst for the family's self-examination at a time of social shifts in the South and political ones on the world stage.

Publisher: Dramatists Play Service

The Whipping Man   Matthew Lopez

Set in Virginia in the period shortly after the Civil War, a wounded Confederate soldier returns to his father's home, still occupied by two of his family's former slaves. Family secrets are revealed as the three men prepare for Passover.

Publisher: Samuel French

FOB   Henry David Hwang

Shifting between a modern day narrative and Chinese myths, two Asian American cousins confront their attitudes about their Chinese heritage when they encounter a recently arrived exchange student at their Los Angeles college. The play draws on details from several Chinese myths, including *Fa Mu Lan* and *Gwan Gung*.

Publisher: Dramatists Play Service

A Shayna Maidel   Barbara Lebow

Two sisters are separated during World War II: one emigrates to America with their father; the other remains in Poland with their mother. Sixteen years later the two sisters are reunited. Memories of a lost mother linger in the mind of the Holocaust survivor in the form of flashbacks.

Publisher: Dramatists Play Service

Skeleton Crew   Dominique Morisseau

Four workers in a Detroit stamping plant face the possible closing of their factory. Between their shifts, the shop steward, foreman, a pregnant worker, and the crew's "big mouth" share their struggles, fears, and secrets as they consider the personal and economic impact of the eroding American auto industry.

Publisher: Doollee.com

Anna in the Tropics   Nilo Cruz

Cigar factory workers in Ybor City section of Tampa, Florida listen to great works of literature being read during their shift. In the late 1920s, a new lector comes to the factory as that tradition wanes and the factory is faced with adopting new automated manufacturing techniques. As the lector reads *Anna Karenina*, it serves as a catalyst for the workers' professional and personal choices.

Publisher: Dramatists Play Service

Harmless   Brett Neveu

A college student, returned from his service in Iraq, submits a graphic story to his creative writing teacher based on his military experiences, which sets off an investigation into whether that student poses a threat to his Midwestern campus or not. This play is part of a trilogy about the aftermath of the Iraq War that includes another play, *Old Glory*, also accessible to students.

Publisher: Broadway Play Publishing, Inc.

Adaptations of Fiction and Non-fiction

The Diary of Anne Frank   Wendy Kesselman, from Frances Goodrich
                                              and Albert Hackett's stage play

This new adaptation of Anne Frank's diary presents her story of her confinement in the attic with her family by incorporating newly discovered excerpts from her diary as well as information from other survivors.

Publisher: Dramatists Play Service
Film adaptation: 1959, directed by George Stevens based on Goodrich and Hackett's play

To Kill A Mockingbird   Christopher Sergel from Harper Lee

Using this widely produced stage adaptation alongside reading the novel literally allows students to follow Atticus Finch's advice to put themselves "into [another person's] skin and walk around in it." Sergel's adaptation is available in full length and one act versions.

Publisher of both versions: Dramatic Play Service
Film adaptation: 1962, directed by Alan J. Pakula

My Name Is Asher Lev   Aaron Posner from Chiam Potok

Asher discovers his artistic gift as an adolescent. He must negotiate following his passion to paint culturally challenging images with his parents' religious activism both in their Hasidic community in Brooklyn and abroad before, during, and after World War II.

Publisher: Dramatists Play Service

The Hundred Dresses   Mary Hall Surface from Eleanor Estes

In the 1930s, Wanda, a Polish immigrant girl, must endure the taunts and teasing of her peers. Maddie, one of Wanda's classmates, who initially does not intervene to stop the bullying, learns to stand up the tormenters, who happen to be Maddie's friends.

Publisher: Dramatic Publishing

Metamorphoses: A Play   Mary Zimmerman from Ovid

Zimmerman's acclaimed adaptation of Ovid provides a series of 11 tales, including the stories of Midas, Orpheus and Eurydice, Narcissus, Phaeton, and Eros and Psyche. Zimmerman's other adaptations include *The Arabian Nights* and *Argonautika*, which are also suitable for classroom study.

Publisher: Samuel French

Native Son   Paul Green (1941) and Nambi E. Kelley (2014) from
Richard Wright

Richard Wright's classic novel has garnered two notable adaptations. Both plays distill essential events and characters involved in the tragic experiences of Bigger Thomas, set in Chicago in the 1930s.

Publisher of both versions: Samuel French
Film adaptation: 1986, directed by Jerrold Freedman

Crime and Punishment   Marilyn Campbell and Curt Columbus
                                              from Fyodor Dostoyevsky

This three-character adaptation focuses on Roskolnikov struggling with the forces of spiritual and civil justice embodied by the prostitute, Sonia, and the detective, Porfiry Petrovitch.

Publisher: Dramatic Publishing Company

The Curious Incident of the
Dog in the Night-Time   Simon Stephens from Mark Haddon

A gifted adolescent with Asperger's syndrome pursues a murder mystery in at small English town in 1998. He not only wants to exonerate himself from the crime, but he wants to chronicle his investigation in meticulous detail and to test his limits interacting with the strangers critical to his detective work.

Publisher: Critical Scripts, A&C Black

The Pitmen Painters   Lee Hall from William Feaver

An adult education class begins as a vehicle to provide a group of miners basic training in art and leads to the formation of the Ashington Group of painters. The play is loosely based on the challenges that the miners turned painters face as they pursue their art.

Publisher: Dramatists Play Service

Just Like Us: The True Story of Four
Mexican Girls Coming of Age in America   Karen Zacarias from Helen Thorpe

Set in Denver, four Latina girls prepare for prom, and more broadly their lives beyond their immediate high school experiences. Their individual opportunities are shaped by whether they are documented or not as well as familial expectations. The play places a journalist (Helen Thorpe) as an observer of the girls' interaction, which retains the documentary nature of its source material.

Publisher: Dramatic Publishing

Companions to Canonical Plays

Clybourne Park   Bruce Norris

Picking up the legacy of the Younger Family from *Raisin in the Sun*, this play
sets its drama in two periods: 1959 and 2009. The conflict in each act centers
on the fate of the sale of a home located in a neighborhood that shifts from
being "all White" to "all Black" in the intervening 50 years.

Publisher: Dramatists Play Service

Dollhouse   Rebecca Gilman

Based on *A Doll's House* by Henrik Ibsen, Nora and Terry live in the Lincoln
Park neighborhood of Chicago and they have all the hallmarks of success,
but Nora's compulsive behavior and scheming pushes her into confronting
the dishonesty and deception that lies at the heart of her marriage and her
personal autonomy.

Publisher: Northwestern University Press

Electricidad   Luis Alfaro

Set in an East Los Angeles Chicano barrio, this play adapts Sophocles' *Electra*,
maintaining the elements of a daughter's longing for revenge, a brother's
return from exile, and a violent, tragic confrontation with their mother.

Publisher: Dramatic Publishing

Another Antigone   A.R. Gurney

When a college student submits her anti-nuclear version of the tragedy of
Antigone instead of the required literary analysis paper to her theater professor, a battle of wills escalates over following established academic authority
rather than authentic artistic expression.

Publisher: Dramatists Play Service

The Island   Athol Fugard, John Kani, Winston Ntshona

In apartheid-era South Africa, two prisoners rehearse scenes from Sophocles'
Antigone at night in their cell after their day of performing punishing

physical labor. As the production of the play draws near, one of the prisoners learns of his release. The drama uses the Greek tragedy as a vehicle to explore the plight of political prisoners imprisoned much like the experiences of Nelson Mandela on Robben Island.

Publisher: Samuel French

The Dresser   Ronald Harwood

During World War II, a touring company of actors struggles to perform their repertory slate of Shakespearean plays amid bombing raids, as their aging actor/manager, Sir, struggles to maintain his grip on reality. His dresser, Norman, alternately cajoles and goads him into his final performance of *King Lear*. The relationships between Sir, his dresser, and his company mirror those in Shakespeare's great tragedy.

Publisher: Samuel French
Film adaptations: 1983, directed by Peter Yates; 2015, directed by Richard Eyre for BBC Two

Rosencrantz and Guildenstern are Dead   Tom Stoppard

Hamlet's college friends become the central characters in Stoppard's playful reimagining of Shakespeare's tragedy. Rosencrantz and Guildenstern observe the comings, goings, and protestations of Hamlet, Gertrude, Claudius, et al. They muse about the nature of fate as they engage in verbal tennis matches and games of chance.

Publisher: Grove Press
Film adaptation: 1990, directed by Tom Stoppard

School for Lies   David Ives

This verse play adapts Moliere's *The Misanthrope* adding modern commentary and anachronistic quips to the classic seventeenth-century satire skewering virtue, honesty, hypocrisy, and all manner of human foibles among the moneyed class. Ives excels in inventive wordplay that mimics the original text, while embellishing it with contemporary insights to reveal its universal nature.

Publisher: Dramatic Play Service

A Tempest   Aimé Césaire

Billed as "based on Shakespeare's *The Tempest* for a Black Theater," this adaptation expands its source material's themes of the damaging effects of colonialism to explore and advance the concepts of Negritude popularized in the late 1960s. A power struggle between Prospero, Ariel, and Caliban comes to the foreground.

Publisher: Theater Communications Group

Titles for Interdisciplinary Units

The Crucible   Arthur Miller

Set in colonial Salem, Massachusetts, this well-known drama involving the accusations, trials, and execution of alleged of witches in the midst of a pious Puritan community can set the stage for examining the McCarthy era in an American history class or a variety of topics covered in sociology and psychology curricula.

Publisher: Dramatists Play Service
Film adaptation: 1994 directed by Nicholas Hytner

Not About Nightingales   Tennessee Williams

Based on an incident in a Pennsylvania prison, Williams wrote this play in 1938 and it remained "forgotten" until actress Vanessa Redgrave rediscovered it. In this drama, a group of inmates stage a hunger strike in hopes of improving the conditions in the prison.

Publisher: Samuel French

Inherit the Wind   Jerome Lawrence and Robert Edwin Lee

The Scopes "Monkey" Trial famously put a Southern science teacher's ability to present Darwin's theory of evolution in place of creationist theory.

Publisher: Dramatists Play Service
Film adaptations: 1960, directed by Stanley Kramer; 1988, directed by David Green for TV; 1999, directed by Daniel Petrie for TV

Butler   Richard Strand

Lawyer Benjamin Franklin Butler found himself the Major General of a Union fort in Virginia and with a number of runaway slaves seeking asylum. Butler famously circumvented the "Runaway Slave Act" in a most ingenious manner to prevent the return of the slaves who would most certainly face death if returned to their owners.

Publisher: Doolee.com

Elliot, A Soldier's Fugue   Quiara Algeria Hudes

Set to the music of Bach, the film presents four stories of members of a single Puerto Rican family who served in Iraq, Vietnam, and Korea as well as those who maintained the home front in Philadelphia.

Publisher: Dramatists Play Service

The Best Man   Gore Vidal

Debuting on Broadway in 1960, this play about a presidential primary that pits an ethical candidate against an unethical opponent seems to find new life in most election cycles. Vidal models his characters on both the notable and the notorious politicians of the times.

Publisher: Dramatists Play Service
Film adaptation: 1964, directed by Franklin J. Schaffner

The Triangle Factory Fire Project   Christopher Piehler in collaboration
                                                        with Scott Alan Evans

The Triangle factory fire stands as a watershed event that focused attention on the sweat shop conditions that women faced who worked in the garment district in New York. This "docudrama" approach presents the investigation and legal proceedings which followed the tragedy.

Publisher: Dramatists Play Service

My Kind of Town   John Conroy

The south side of Chicago is the setting to tell this timely story of racial profiling and police torture, and how it affects both the profiling police officers and the profiled young man.

Publisher: Chicago Dramaworks

Inana   Michele Lowe

An Iraqi museum curator brings his bride and a smuggled artifact to London on the brink of the American invasion of Baghdad. The play uses flashbacks to trace what put both the curator's wife and the artifact in peril if they remained in Iraq. The intersecting conflicts address how a culture preserves and honors its heritage while evolving toward a more progressive future.

Publisher: Samuel French

General from America   Richard Nelson

The circumstances that motivated Benedict Arnold to become one of America's most infamous traitors involve high-stakes conflicts among the ambitious and fractious "founding fathers" and within Arnold's own household.

Publisher: Samuel French

Spinning into Butter   Rebecca Gilman

Racism and political correctness are put to the test in a small, mostly White, liberal New England college. The new Dean of Students must confront a shocking hate crime targeting an African-American undergrad as well as face her own entrenched racial prejudices.

Publisher: Dramatic Publishing
Film adaptation: 2007, directed by Mark Brokaw

The Laramie Project   Moisés Kaufman, et al.

Based on a collection of interviews conducted by the Tectonic Theatre Project, the play explores the aftermath and impact of the homophobic murder of Matthew Shepard in Laramie, Wyoming in 1998.

Publisher: Dramatists Play Service
Film adaptation: 2002, directed by Moisés Kaufman

A Man for All Seasons   Robert Bolt

Thomas More famously refused to sign a petition to request the Pope to annul Henry VIII's marriage to Catherine of Aragon so the King could marry Anne

Boleyn. This biographical play dramatizes More resisting efforts on all fronts to persuade him to support not only Henry's remarriage but also recognize his position as Supreme Head of the Church of England.

Publisher: Vintage
Film adaptation: 1966, directed by Fred Zinnermann

Texts for Honors and AP Curricula

Arcadia   Tom Stoppard

Set in an English country house, the plot moves between the early 1800s and the present day. Two characters in the present are conducting separate research projects on events that took place involving the residents of the estate from 1809 to 1812 that concern a lost chapter in the life of Lord Byron and the identity of a mysterious hermit, who lived on the grounds.

Publisher: Faber & Faber UK, Samuel French

The Caretaker   Harold Pinter

A homeless man, Davies, is brought into the home of two brothers, Astin and Mick. An enigmatic power struggle emerges, as Davies pits the two brothers against each other.

The play develops themes of fantasy versus reality and the nature of family relationships.

Publisher: Faber & Faber UK, Dramatists Play Service
Film adaptation: 1964, directed by Clive Donner

Gem of the Ocean   August Wilson

In 1904, Citizen Barlow comes to Pittsburgh from Alabama and to Aunt Ester, a 285-year-old soul cleanser. Citizen meets Solly Two Kings, a former slave and scout for the Union Army there. Both men are seeking redemption and the chance at a new life in the North until a tragic death requires one of them to assume a new responsibility to serve the African American community making their way north.

Publisher: Theatre Communications Group

Angels in America   Tony Kushner

This epic two part play, set in America in the 1980s, focuses on two couples, one gay and one straight, as well as Roy Cohn, who was part of Sen., Joseph McCarthy's HUAC team in the 1950s. The play's action moves through a series of fantastic dream sequences experienced by various characters as a result of their illness, drug addiction, or personal anxiety.

Publisher: Theater Communications Group
Film adaptation: 2003, directed by Mike Nichols

August Osage County   Tracy Letts

A father's suicide and a mother's ill health and drug addiction set the stage for a multi-generational family reunion bathed in confessions and betrayals that are both darkly comedic and bitterly tragic. A Native American woman hired by the family patriarch shortly before his death, to act as a live-in cook and caregiver for his wife, quietly observes with a copy of T. S. Eliot in hand.

Publisher: Dramatists Play Service, Theater Communications Group
Film adaptation: 2014, directed by John Wells

The Seagull   Anton Chekhov

A Russian country estate hosts the performance of a play that brings together the playwright, an aspiring young actress, a stage diva, and her lover. The artistic aspirations and romantic entanglements provoke immediate decisions that lead to regret, disappointment, and tragic consequences both at the time and three years later when characters are reunited.

Publisher: Dramatists Play Service (Christopher Hampton, translator), among other translations
Film adaptations: 2016, directed by Michael Mayer; as *The Sea Gull* 1968, directed by Sidney Lumet

An Enemy of the People   Henrik Ibsen

A doctor discovers that a local bathhouse/spa is contaminating the town's water supply. His revelation is initially met with praise but ultimately puts the doctor at odds with the town officials, including his own brother, who fear the town's economy is threatened by shutting down the baths. The doctor's motives and reputation ultimately come under attack.

Publisher: Dramatists Play Service (adapted for the American stage by Arthur Miller), Samuel French (translated by Christopher Hampton), among other translations
Film adaptation: 1978, directed by George Schaefer from Miller's adaptation

M Butterfly   David Henry Hwang

Inspired by Puccini's opera and based on actual events, the play chronicles a French diplomat's affair over 20 years with a Chinese opera singer he believes to be a woman but who is actually a man. The play is not prurient in approach to the narrative; rather it focuses on the power of illusion and the potent fallacies of Western Imperialism.

Publisher: Plume, Dramatists Play Service
Film Adaptation: 1993, directed by David Cronenberg

The History Boys   Alan Bennett

Students in a boarding school in northern England prepare for entrance exams that would admit them to Cambridge or Oxford universities under the supervision of three teachers, with drastically different instructional styles. The school community discovers that one of the teachers has fondled a student.

Publisher: Samuel French
Film adaptation: 2006, directed by Nicholas Hytner

Eurydice   Sara Ruhl

This is a postmodern adaptation of the Eurydice myth that focuses on Eurydice's decision to return to earth with Orpheus or to stay in the Underworld to remain with her father.

Publisher: Samuel French

Appendix C: Recommended Resources

Boal, Augusto. *Games for Actors and Non-Actors*. 2nd ed. Trans. Adrian Jackson. New York: Routledge, 1999. Print.

Bolton, Gavin. *Acting in Classroom Drama: An Analysis*. Portsmouth, NH: Heinemann, 1993. Print.

Doona, John. *Secondary Drama: A Source Book*. New York: Routledge, 2014. Print.

Edmiston, Brian. *Transforming Teaching and Learning with Active and Dramatic Approaches: Engaging Students Across the Curriculum*. New York: Routledge, 2013. Print.

Gallagher, Kelly. *Readicide: How Schools Are Killing Reading and What You Can Do About It*. Portland, ME: Stenhouse, 2009. Print.

Spolin, Viola. *Improvisation for the Theater: A Handbook of Teaching and Directing Techniques*. 3rd ed. Evanston, IL: Northwestern University Press, 1999. Print.

Wessling, Sarah Brown, Daneille Lillge, and Crystal VanKooten. *Supporting Students in a Time of Core Standards: English Language Arts Grades 9–12*. Urbana, IL: National Council of Teachers of English, 2011. Print.

Bibliography

Altman, Josh. *My Name Is Asher Lev*: *Dramaturgical Packet*. Chicago: TimeLine Theatre Company, 2014. Print.

Edutopia. *Rubric for Speech*. n.d. Web. 31 Mar. 2016.

Gardner, Howard. *Frames of Mind: The Theory of Multiple Intelligences*. 2nd ed. New York: Basic Books, 1993. Print.

Hansberry, Lorraine. *A Raisin in the Sun*. New York: Vintage, 1994. Print.

Hughes, Langston. "Harlem." *Selected Poems of Langston Hughes*. New York: Random House, Inc., 1990. Print.

——. "Mother To Son." *The Collected Poems of Langston Hughes*. New York: Vintage Books, 1994. Print.

Links, Alexis Jade. *A Raisin in the Sun*: Dramaturgical Packet. Chicago: TimeLine Theatre Company, 2013. Print.

Marino, Kelli. *"Master Harold" and the boys*: *Dramaturgical Packet*. Chicago: TimeLine Theatre Company, 2010. Print.

McKnight, Katherine and Mary Scruggs. *The Second City Guide to Improv in the Classroom: Using Improvisation to Teach Skills and Improve Learning*. San Francisco: Jossey-Bass, 2008. Print.

Miller, Arthur. *The Crucible*. NY: Penguin/Random House, 2003. Print.

National Council of Teachers of English and International Literacy Association. *ReadWriteThink*. n.d. Web. 31 Mar. 2016.

Robinson, Maren. *Inana*: *Dramaturgical Packet*. Chicago: TimeLine Theatre Company, 2015. Print.

Royal Shakespeare Company. *The RSC Shakespeare Toolkit for Teachers: An Active Approach to Bringing Shakespeare's Plays Alive in the Classroom*. Revised ed. London: Metheun, 2013. Print.

Spolin, Viola. *Theater Games for the Classroom: A Teacher's Handbook*. Evanston, IL: Northwestern University Press, 1986. Print.

Sugarman, Robert. *Performing Shakespeare: A Way to Learn*. Shaftsbury, VT: Mountainside Press, 2005. Print.

Theater Communications Group. *Building A National TEAM: Theatre Education*. n.d. Web. 31 Mar. 2016.

The News Manual. *A Professional Resource for Journalists and The Media*. n.d. Web. 31 Mar. 2016.

Tovani, Cris. *I Read It, But I Don't Get It: Comprehension Strategies for Adolescent Readers*. Portland, ME: Stenhouse Publishers, 2000. Print.

University of Illinois at Urbana-Champaign. "Physical Activity May Strengthen Children's Ability To Pay Attention." *Science Daily*. 1 April 2009. Web. 31 Mar. 2016.